D1316257

REMEMBER,
REMEMBER
(THE FIFTH OF NOVEMBER)

Also by Judy Parkinson

i before e (except after c)

REMEMBER, REMEMBER
(THE FIFTH OF NOVEMBER)

Everything You've Ever Wanted to
Know About British History with
All the Boring Bits Taken Out

JUDY PARKINSON

DELACORTE PRESS

Published in the United States by Delacorte Press,
an imprint of The Random House Publishing Group,
a division of Random House, Inc., New York.

DELACORTE PRESS is a registered trademark of Random House, Inc., and the
colophon is a trademark of Random House, Inc.

Originally published in Great Britain by
Michael O'Mara Books Limited in 2008.

Library of Congress Cataloging-in-Publication Data

Parkinson, Judy.
Remember, remember (The Fifth of November) : everything you've
ever wanted to know about British history with all the boring bits
taken out / Judy Parkinson.
p.   cm.
"First published in Great Britain in 2008 by
Michael O'Mara books"—T.p. verso.
Includes bibliographical references and index.
ISBN 978-0-385-34364-0
1. Great Britain—History—Chronology. 2. Great Britain—History—
Outlines, syllabi, etc. I. Title.
DA34.P37 2009
941.002'02—dc22
2009020780

Printed in the United States of America on acid-free paper

www.bantamdell.com

2 4 6 8 9 7 5 3 1

First Edition

Book design by www.glensaville.com

CONTENTS

Tudor Britain

Stuart Britain

Georgian Britain

Victorian Britain

Edwardian Britain

The First World War Years

The Interwar Years

The Second World War

For Grandpa
December 7, 1889–December 18, 1977

Driver RJ Barrett, Royal Field Artillery
Regimental number 9863
Served in France and Italy
Military Medal awarded October 28, 1918

EDITORS' INTRODUCTION AND ACKNOWLEDGMENTS

This book was born out of a desire to encapsulate the whole sweep of British history— from the Roman invasion to the end of the Second World War—in no more than 150 entries, each no longer than 250 words. Could it be done? At first, the task seemed impossible: How could something as complex as the Wars of the Roses or the Treaty of Versailles possibly be condensed into such a brief entry? But after much painstaking (and painful) pruning, the result is, we believe, a comprehensive overview that gives you all the key facts without any flab.

Why we undertook this task is another matter. For many of us, Britain's history was taught piecemeal, with in-depth coverage of some periods and complete absence of information on others. For some, perhaps an older generation, it was taught as a list of worthy but dull dates, which were very easily forgotten. It is not surprising, therefore, that many of us reach adulthood with embarrassing gaps in our knowledge, conscious of a vague feeling that we should know more about the subject. Which George was which? Was Bloody Mary the same as Mary, Queen of Scots? And who murdered Thomas à Becket, and why did it matter anyway?

This is where *Remember, Remember* steps in. Aiming to address these gaps in a simple, accessible format, each subject is presented as a short, self-contained "article," designed to be dipped into, yet both comprehensive and accurate. An index is provided for cross-reference purposes—history is nothing if not interlinked—and a list of further reading. There is also a list of monarchs and an extended time line, covering most major events including those that, for reasons of space, do not have their own entries in the main text.

In short, this book will provide you with a useful introduction to and overview of British history, though if you want a detailed analysis of the effects of the repeal of the Corn Laws on nineteenth-century foreign trade you will, sadly, need to look elsewhere.

Like all the best and most enthralling stories, this country's history is a tale of courage and character, honor and faith, pride and hope, skill and invention, endurance and, sometimes, sheer luck. *Remember, Remember* restores us to the glorious—and, often, not so glorious—narrative of these islands' story, and on the way reminds us of what we've forgotten, or teaches us what we were never taught.

The editors would like to thank, first of all, the author, Judy Parkinson, for her sterling research work and efficiency under extreme time pressure. We would also like to thank Dominique Enright and Jamie Buchan for their meticulous fact-checking, Ana Bjezancevic for the lovely cover design and map, and Claire and Toby Buchan for Britannia and much besides. Grateful thanks are also due to Thomas Edlin, historian at Westminster, for his thorough attention to detail and hugely helpful insights, and Dr. Frances Ramsey, also of Westminster School, for putting us on to him. Needless to say, any remaining mistakes are our own.

TIME LINE

ROMAN BRITAIN

55 and 54 B.C.	Roman incursions of Julius Caesar
A.D. 47	Conquest of southeast England
50	Founding of Londinium
60/61	Revolt of Queen Boudicca
70–84	Conquest of Wales and Scotland
122	Hadrian's Wall built
196–213	Britain becomes two provinces
306	Constantine the Great proclaimed at York
367–369	Barbarian offensive
398–400	Victories over Picts, Scots, Saxons

THE DARK AGES

477	Saxon settlement of Sussex
495	Saxon settlement of Wessex
597	Saint Augustine lands in Kent
664	Synod of Whitby
731	The Venerable Bede completes his *History*
757	Offa becomes King of Mercia
793	Danish raids on Lindisfarne, Jarrow, Iona
865	Danish (Viking) army lands
867	Northumbria falls to the Danes
871	Danes attack Wessex, Alfred becomes king
878	Alfred defeats Danes at Edington
910–920	Most of the Danelaw recaptured
991	Treaty between England and Normandy
1002	Ethelred orders massacre of Danes in England
1017	King Canute divides England into four earldoms
1042	Edward the Confessor becomes king
1066	Battle of Hastings

1086	Domesday Survey
1120	White Ship sinks—Henry I's heir dies
1139–1153	Civil war in England
1153	Henry of Anjou (Henry II) invades England
1169–1172	English conquest of Ireland begins
1170	Murder of Thomas à Becket
1190–1192	Richard I on Crusade
1215	Magna Carta, civil war in England
1258	Barons take over royal government
1259	Treaty of Paris between England and France
1264	Battle of Lewes, Simon de Montfort's government
1282–1283	Edward I's conquest of Wales
1291	Edward I becomes overlord of Scotland
1294	War with France begins
1295	Franco-Scottish alliance
1296	Edward I invades Scotland
1306	Robert the Bruce's rebellion
1314	Scottish victory at Bannockburn
1315–1317	Great Famine
1337	Hundred Years War begins
1346	English victory at the Battle of Crécy
1347	English capture Calais
1348	Black Death arrives in England
1356	English defeat French at Poitiers
1381	Peasants' Revolt
1382	John Wycliffe's Bible condemned
1389	Richard II comes of age
1399	Richard II deposed by Henry IV
1415	English victory at Agincourt
1419–1420	English conquest of Normandy
1449–1450	French overrun Normandy
1455	Battle of St. Albans—start of the Wars of the Roses

1477	William Caxton's first printed book
1483	Richard III becomes king, deposing his nephew Edward V
1485	Richard III killed at Bosworth, Henry VII becomes king

TUDOR BRITAIN

1509	Henry VIII becomes king
1512	War with France and Scotland
1513	English defeat Scots at Battle of Flodden
1522–1525	War with France
1527	Divorce crisis begins
1528	War with Spain
1533	Henry VIII marries Anne Boleyn
1534	The first Act of Supremacy
1536–1540	The dissolution of the monasteries
1542	English defeat Scots at Battle of Solway Moss
1543	War with France
1549	First Book of Common Prayer
1553	Mary I becomes queen after Lady Jane Grey's "Nine Days"
1555	Persecution of Protestants begins
1556	Cranmer burned at the stake
1557	War with France
1558	Calais taken by the French
1558	Elizabeth I becomes queen
1559	Religious settlement in England
1568	Mary, Queen of Scots escapes to England
1569	Northern Rebellion
1584	Virginia starts to be colonized
1585	War with Spain
1587	Execution of Mary, Queen of Scots
1588	Defeat of the Spanish Armada
1601	Rebellion of the Earl of Essex
1603	Elizabeth I dies

STUART BRITAIN

1603	James VI of Scotland becomes James I of England
1604	Peace with Spain
1605	The Gunpowder Plot
1611	King James Bible published
1620	The Pilgrim Fathers sail to New England
1624–1630	War with Spain
1626–1629	War with France
1629	Charles I dissolves Parliament and starts eleven years of "Personal Rule"
1630	Emigration to Massachusetts begins
1640	Long Parliament called
1642	English Civil War begins
1644	Parliamentary victory at the Battle of Marston Moor
1645	Parliamentary armies become the New Model Army and win at Naseby
1648	Second Civil War
1649	Trial and execution of Charles I, England becomes a Republic
1649–1650	Oliver Cromwell conquers Ireland
1650–1652	Cromwell conquers Scotland
1652–1654	First Dutch War
1653	Cromwell becomes Lord Protector
1658	Cromwell dies
1660	Restoration of the monarchy, Charles II crowned
1665–1667	Second Dutch War
1665	Great Plague
1666	Great Fire of London
1672–1674	Third Dutch War
1678	Titus Oates and the Popish Plot
1679	Habeas Corpus Act passed
1679–1681	Emergence of Whig and Tory parties

1685	Monmouth Rebellion
1688	William of Orange invades and James II flees
1689	William and Mary crowned
1689	Bill of Rights
1690	Battle of the Boyne
1694	Bank of England founded
1701	Act of Settlement lays out Hanoverian succession
1704	Battle of Blenheim
1707	Union of England and Scotland

GEORGIAN BRITAIN

1714	George I becomes king
1715	Jacobite Rebellion
1720	South Sea Bubble
1721	Robert Walpole's ministry begins
1733	Excise Crisis
1739	War of Jenkins's Ear, Anglo-Spanish naval war
1745	Bonnie Prince Charlie leads Jacobite Rebellion
1746	Battle of Culloden
1752	Adoption of Gregorian Calendar
1756–1763	Seven Years War
1757	Battle of Plassey
1759–1760	Annus Mirabilis, the Year of Victories
1759	Capture of Quebec, France defeated
1760	George III becomes king
1769	James Watt's steam engine
1773	Boston Tea Party
1776	Declaration of American Independence
1781	Americans defeat British at Yorktown
1783	American colonies become independent
1783	Pitt the Younger becomes prime minister
1784	East India Act
1789	Mutiny on the *Bounty*
1789	French Revolution
1791	Thomas Paine's *Rights of Man* published

1793	War with France
1798	First introduction of income tax
1799	Napoleon appointed First Consul of France
1801	The Act of Union between Britain and Ireland and first UK Parliament
1802	Peace with France
1803	War with France
1805	The Battle of Trafalgar and death of Nelson
1807	Abolition of the slave trade
1811–1812	The Luddite riots
1811	George, Prince of Wales made Prince Regent
1815	The Battle of Waterloo, Napoleon defeated
1819	Peterloo Massacre
1820	George IV becomes king
1821–1823	Famine in Ireland
1829	Catholics gain civil rights (emancipation)
1832	Great Reform Act
1833	Slavery abolished in British colonies
1834	Grand National Consolidated Trade Union founded

VICTORIAN BRITAIN

1837	Queen Victoria becomes Queen
1839	Chartist riots
1840	Penny post introduced
1845–1852	Irish potato famine
1846	Abolition of the Corn Laws
1851	Great Exhibition
1854–1856	Crimean War
1857–1858	Indian Mutiny
1859	Charles Darwin publishes *The Origin of Species*
1861	Prince Albert dies
1869	Suez Canal opens
1870	Irish Land Act
1877	Victoria becomes Empress of India
1880–1881	First Boer War

1882	Britain occupies Egypt
1885	Death of Gordon at Khartoum
1886	First Home Rule Bill for Ireland (defeated)
1891	Education Act
1893	Independent Labour Party founded
1896–1898	Sudan conquered
1898	German naval expansion
1899–1902	Second Boer War
1900	Salisbury wins Khaki Election
1901	Queen Victoria dies, Edward VII becomes king

EDWARDIAN BRITAIN

1902	Balfour's Education Act
1903	First Lib-Lab Pact
1904	Anglo-French *Entente Cordiale*
1905	Title "Prime Minister" acquires formal status
1908	Prime Minister Asquith introduces Old Age Pension
1911	Parliament Act limits power of the lords
1912	The sinking of the *Titanic*

THE FIRST WORLD WAR YEARS

1914	Assassination of Archduke Franz Ferdinand at Sarajevo, British Empire enters First World War
1915–1916	Dardanelles expedition, withdrawal from Gallipoli
1916	Easter Rising, Dublin
1916	Battle of the Somme
1916	David Lloyd George becomes prime minister
1917	Battle of Passchendaele
1918	Flu pandemic starts
1918	Women granted limited rights to vote
1919	Treaty of Versailles, League of Nations established

THE INTERWAR YEARS

1919	Amritsar Massacre, India
1920	British Mandate for Palestine and Mesopotamia
1921	Anglo-Irish Peace Treaty and Partition of Ireland, Irish Free State established
1924	First Labour Government
1926	General Strike
1928	Women get the vote on equal footing with men
1929	Ramsay MacDonald leads second Labour Government
1931	Financial crisis: National Government
1936	George V dies, Edward VIII abdicates, George VI becomes king
1938	Chamberlain meets Hitler at Munich

THE SECOND WORLD WAR

1939	Germany invades Poland, British Empire declares war against Germany
1940	Winston Churchill succeeds Chamberlain as prime minister
1940	British withdrawal from Dunkirk
1940	Battle of Britain
1940–1941	Luftwaffe Blitz on Britain
1941	America and Russia enter the war
1942	Loss of Singapore
1942	Montgomery's victory at El Alamein
1942	Battle of Stalingrad
1942	Beveridge Report on Social Security
1944	D-day landings in Normandy
1945	End of Second World War
1945	Massive Labour victory, Attlee becomes prime minister
1945	Atomic bombs dropped on Japan
1945	United Nations established

LIST OF MONARCHS

1272–1307	Edward I (Longshanks)
1307–1327	Edward II (of Caernarvon)
1327–1377	Edward III
1377–1399	Richard II (of Bordeaux)

HOUSE OF LANCASTER

1399–1413	Henry IV (of Bolingbroke)
1413–1422	Henry V (of Monmouth)
1422–1461	Henry VI (of Windsor)

HOUSE OF YORK

1461–1483	Edward IV
1483	Edward V
1483–1485	Richard III

HOUSE OF TUDOR

1485–1509	Henry VII
1509–1547	Henry VIII
1547–1553	Edward VI
1553	Lady Jane Grey
1553–1558	Mary I
1558–1603	Elizabeth I

HOUSE OF STUART

| 1603–1625 | James VI/I |
| 1625–1649 | Charles I |

INTERREGNUM

| 1649–1660 | Commonwealth and Protectorate |

HOUSE OF STUART

1660–1685	Charles II
1685–1688	James II
1689–1702	William III and Mary II (*d.* 1694)
1702–1714	Anne

HOUSE OF HANOVER

1714–1727	George I
1727–1760	George II
1760–1820	George III

1820–1830	George IV
1830–1837	William IV
1837–1901	Victoria

HOUSE OF SAXE-COBURG AND GOTHA

1901–1910	Edward VII

HOUSE OF WINDSOR

1910–1936	George V
1936	Edward VIII
1936–1952	George VI
1952–	Elizabeth II

ROMAN BRITAIN

THE ROMAN INVASION
A.D. 43

The Romans were empire builders on a mission to spread their civilization to barbarian lands. One such was Britain, which consisted of various unruly Celtic tribes in conflict with each other (a situation the Romans exploited). Julius Caesar's attempts, in 55 and 54 B.C., to occupy Britain were defeated by bad weather. Augustus threatened, but never carried out, invasions in 34, 27 and 25 B.C. In A.D. 43, the unpopular Emperor Claudius needed to improve his image in Rome; an invasion of Britain would bring favorable publicity.

The Romans landed on the south coast—possibly Kent—and swept through the south, with fierce fighting that drove the British northwest. By A.D. 50, eleven tribes had surrendered and southern Britain was Romanized. Camulodunum (modern Colchester) was the first capital, but the Romans soon saw the potential of the Thames and established Londinium as a commercial and administrative center at the hub of a road network. London soon became capital of the new province, Britannia.

Partial domination of the west came with a Welsh campaign in A.D. 54–60, though Boudicca's rebellion in East Anglia delayed occupation. Northward expansion was more problematic, and despite several efforts Scotland was never wholly conquered.

The influence of occupation on British culture was enormous. Roman customs, laws and religions were adopted, while the Romans introduced such facilities as public baths and exercise areas, underfloor central heating and a road system on which today's network is loosely based.

THE FOUNDING OF LONDINIUM
c. A.D. 50

Before the Roman invasion of A.D. 43, the site of London was a marshy patch of wasteland through which the River Thames flowed. As the Romans advanced northward, they came to a point where they could ford the river. A fort was built on the north side, and work began on a network of roads.

With the river's usefulness as means of transport and its wide estuary facing the European mainland, the region's potential was not lost on the Romans. A bridge was built, and settlers, mainly traders, began to arrive. Slowly a town, Londinium, grew up around them.

It was not safe, however, and when Boudicca's Iceni tribe rose up against the Romans, the governor of Britannia, Suetonius Paulinus, displayed cool leadership, urging the citizens of Londinium to flee. Those who could not were slaughtered, and the town was razed by the angry Britons.

Apart from a quay, little was built on the site for some twenty years, but then began a period of spectacular growth, and by about A.D. 120, Londinium had established itself as the administrative, commercial and financial center of Roman Britain. A major fire in the following decade marked the start of a setback, but it still remained a wealthy and important Roman stronghold, as revealed by the remains of large and fine Roman villas found in the city area and the great defensive wall built around the city between A.D. 190 and 225.

QUEEN BOUDICCA
d. A.D. 60/61

A Briton woman of the royal family . . . In stature she was very tall, in appearance most terrifying, in the glance of her eye most fierce, and her voice was harsh; a great mass of the tawniest hair fell to her hips; around her neck was a large golden necklace . . ." (The Roman historian Cassius Dio on Boudicca, some 150 years after her death).

When the Romans invaded Britain in A.D. 43, they allowed some tribal rulers to remain as "client kings" under the Roman emperor. One such was Prasutagus, who ruled the Iceni (in the East Anglia region) with his queen, Boudicca. When he died in A.D. 60, the Romans ignored his will, which left the kingdom to his daughters jointly with the Roman emperor, and instead took control themselves. For good measure they publicly flogged Boudicca and raped her daughters.

In response, Boudicca mustered the support of other English tribes and rose up against the Romans. From her chariot, her daughters at her side, she led an army of some 100,000 men, which destroyed the Roman capital at Camulodunum (Colchester), went on to devastate Londinium and Verulamium (St. Albans), and slaughtered the 9th Roman Legion, despite being vastly outnumbered.

The Romans rallied, however, and eventually defeated Boudicca, perhaps in the West Midlands. Boudicca herself died, having reputedly taken poison. Nothing is known of the fate of her daughters.

HADRIAN'S WALL
A.D. 122–130

Hadrian's Wall was a seventy-three-mile fifteen-foot-high wall built by the Romans under the Emperor Hadrian to separate the barbarians in Scotland (Britannia Inferior, as the Romans called it) from the newly civilized Britons to the south (Britannia Superior), and to prevent raids from the north. Its height made it useful for surveillance as well as defense. Stretching from Wallsend-on-Tyne to the Solway Firth, it marked the northern boundary of the Empire and influenced the position of the current Scottish border.

The wall consisted of a stone wall with a ditch or *vallum* to the south, interspersed with a number of forts. It was built by skilled members of the Roman army, who took pride in being part of the greatest civilizing force of all time, as well as local people who would benefit from the increased security and economic stability the wall would bring. Settlements soon sprang up nearby.

Under Antoninus Pius, further attempts to conquer Scotland led to the construction of the heavily fortified Antonine Wall one hundred miles north in 138–142. Antoninus could never completely conquer the Scottish tribes, however, and the border returned to Hadrian's Wall from 164 until the end of Roman occupation.

Hadrian's Wall was one of the most sophisticated border posts in the Roman world; an icon of security to Britannia Superior. Despite having been plundered for building materials over the centuries, parts of the wall remain today and it is a popular walking area.

SAINT ALBAN
A.D. mid–200s

Saint Alban was England's first Christian martyr. A pagan living in Verulamium (now St. Albans) during a period of vicious Roman persecution against Christians, Alban offered refuge to Amphibolus, a Christian cleric on the run, and was so impressed by Amphibolus's belief that he converted and was baptized. Alban then made the ultimate sacrifice and, disguising himself in his guest's cloak, gave himself up in his stead (though this hardly helped Amphibolus, who was caught and stoned to death days later).

The story has various associated legends—most famously, his executioner's eyes are said to have fallen out in an act of divine retribution. As he was about to be beheaded Alban declared, "I worship and adore the true and living God who created all things." These words are still used in prayer at St. Albans Abbey, which stands on the site of his death.

The accession in 306 of Emperor Constantine I, who converted to Christianity in 312, brought greater religious tolerance. In 313, the Edict of Milan proclaimed protection for Christians throughout the Empire.

Saint Alban is the patron saint of converts, refugees and torture victims. In 2006, a group of Church of England clergy campaigned to replace Saint George with Saint Alban as England's patron saint.

CONSTANTINE THE GREAT
A.D. 272–337

Constantine was the son of the military commander Constantius, who became emperor in 305, and Helena, a woman of humble origins (discarded in favor of a noblewoman when Constantius became emperor). Constantius died while fighting in Britain in 306, and Constantine was declared emperor—but for many years he had to fight off rivals and was not secure in his position until 324. In 312, on the eve of a battle against a rival, Christ appeared to him in a dream and told him to inscribe a sign resembling a cross on his soldiers' shields; a vision followed of a cross against the sun, with the words *In hoc signo vinces* ("In this sign you will conquer"). He did conquer—and converted to Christianity.

Constantine had already been promoting religious tolerance throughout the empire since 306; in 313, he and his co-emperor issued the Edict of Milan ordering that no action should be taken against any religions. The Christian Church, moreover, was granted special benefits.

In 324 Constantine took command of the whole empire, uniting it through Christianity, which he proclaimed the official religion. He built a new capital city, Constantinople, on the site of the ancient Greek city of Byzantium. As the first Christian emperor of Rome, he played a major part in establishing Christianity in Europe, paving the way for it becoming the predominant religion in Britain. (His mother, also Christian and of English extraction, was later remembered as Saint Helena.)

THE DECLINE OF THE ROMANS
A.D. 367

Tribal skirmishes against the Romans were commonplace throughout the four-hundred-year Roman occupation. But until the fourth century A.D., the "barbarians" were kept at bay. Even the Picts of Caledonia were held back north of Hadrian's Wall.

But then came increasing attacks from Germanic invaders in the east, and in 367 Picts and Scotti took advantage of a rebellious garrison on Hadrian's Wall to pour through into Britain. Simultaneously, there came hordes of Saxons from the east, and from the west attacks by the Irish and the Attacotti tribe.

Cities were sacked and civilians raped, murdered or enslaved, as bands of marauders fought and looted their way across Britain. Confusion reigned for many months, but by the end of 368 the barbarians had been driven back. However, the attacks continued, and Angles and Jutes as well as Saxons came over from Germany and Denmark. Some Saxons were even believed to have been invited over by the British warlord Vortigern to act as mercenaries against the Picts, only for them to revolt and establish their own power bases in the southeast. With the Celts driven westward as the Anglo-Saxons settled in the east, a division between what we now know as "England" and "Wales" became apparent for the first time.

Faced with these constant threats in Britain as well as other troublesome parts of Europe, the overstretched Romans pulled out of Britain at the beginning of the fifth century. The remaining Britons rejected the Roman way of life, and Britain rapidly descended into the so-called "Dark Ages."

THE
DARK AGES

THE ADVENT OF THE SAXONS
440s

By the early 400s, the Western Roman Empire was in decline and had effectively withdrawn from Britain. In its place came a new wave of migration: Angles, Saxons and Jutes, belonging to pagan German and Danish tribes. The new invaders, arriving in small boats, found most of the Roman towns abandoned and in ruins. They gradually conquered much of England, spreading from the southeast, and ruled in various forms for about six hundred years. The Roman language, culture and economy declined and most people lived a hand-to-mouth existence. Violence and disease were rife, and slavery was a common fate for anyone hungry or hard up in the Dark Ages.

At first, Christianity withered as the Anglo-Saxons worshipped multiple pagan gods such as Tiw, Wodin, Thunor (later Thor) and Friya, who gave their names to four days of the week. (Sunday and Monday are paganistically named after the sun and moon, but Saturday, after Saturn, retains Roman influence.) The Christian festival of Easter was named after their old pagan goddess Eostre.

The Anglo-Saxon language formed the basis of modern-day English, giving us the word "England" ("Angle-land"), among others. The Anglo-Saxons brought Bible translations, legal works and epic poetry (most famously *Beowulf*) into the British literary tradition. Under their rule, England's diverse kingdoms were slowly unified into a single country for the first time.

SAINT PATRICK
c. 461 or 493

Patrick was born into a wealthy British family, but where and when is uncertain. Although his father was a Christian deacon, Patrick was not initially religious. As a teenager, he was kidnapped by Irish raiders, taken to Ireland and sold into slavery. He worked as a shepherd for six years, finding comfort in religion and eventually seeing his ordeal as divine retribution for his earlier lack of faith. He escaped by stowing away on a boat to Britain, where he became a priest.

But Patrick was inspired by a dream to return to Ireland as a missionary, and he departed after years of study. Despite difficult relations with pagan chiefs, he organized existing Irish Christians and converted many pagans—the snakes he supposedly drove from Ireland probably represented pagan beliefs. Patrick merged Celtic and Christian symbolism, and is traditionally linked with the three-leaved shamrock, which he used to symbolize the Trinity. Patrick was the second Bishop of Ireland, and one of the key figures in spreading Christianity to Western Europe.

By the eighth century, Patrick was the patron saint of Ireland. Saint Patrick's Day is now celebrated on March 17, possibly the day of his death.

SAINT AUGUSTINE OF CANTERBURY
d. 604/605

The Roman Pope (later Saint) Gregory I was eager to expand the Church's influence and eliminate paganism, particularly in England where such beliefs were still dominant. He sent forty monks, led by Augustine, as missionaries to England, and they landed in 597 at Thanet in Kent.

The monks brought gifts for King Ethelbert of Kent, who greeted them cordially, though the pagan king is said to have insisted on outdoor negotiations in case they cast spells on him. Despite this initial mistrust, the king granted Augustine land at Canterbury where he built a monastery. Augustine became the first Archbishop of Canterbury, although it would be decades before British bishops recognized the office and even longer before Canterbury's primacy over the English Church was secured.

Ethelbert's wife Bertha was Christian, and she and Augustine together persuaded Ethelbert to convert. He was the first English king to do so, and inspired thousands of his subjects to follow. The king helped to spread Christianity among the Saxons, and was later canonized himself. Augustine and Ethelbert set up bishoprics in Rochester and London (the first St. Paul's Cathedral).

Many British Christians continued to maintain some Celtic traditions and refused to convert fully to the Roman Catholic Church. Eventually, at the Synod of Whitby in 664, they accepted Roman control and abandoned Celtic practices.

THE VENERABLE BEDE
673–735

Bede was a pioneering British historian, often known as "the Father of English History." He was born in Northumbria, and grew up in a Benedictine monastery at Jarrow. There he benefited from the monastery's extensive library, and was ordained as a deacon at nineteen and a priest at thirty. Bede was a teacher, scholar and prolific writer who specialized in Scripture but also wrote about language, science and poetry.

He is best known for his masterwork, *The Ecclesiastical History of the English People,* completed in 731. Amid sparse and unreliable records, it remains a vital source for the study of the Dark Ages. Bede's research into myths and oral traditions resulted in a comprehensive history that spanned nearly eight hundred years—from Caesar's invasion to its publication—and popularized the A.D./B.C. dating system. King Alfred considered it an essential educational tool, and had the book translated from Latin into English.

Bede died in 735 and was buried in Jarrow. He became known as "Venerable" some time in the century after his death, possibly due to a grammatical error in his epitaph. He was made a Doctor of the Church and canonized in 1899.

OFFA, THE FIRST "KING OF ALL ENGLAND"

d. 796; crowned 757*

The balance of power had changed significantly over the seventh century. The kingdom of Mercia, now in the Midlands, had become dominant, overtaking Northumbria. However, Mercia appears to have suffered internal strife, and when King Ethelbald was murdered by his bodyguard in 757, it triggered a short civil war, which allowed his kinsman Offa to take over and rule over an expansion of Mercian power.

Offa continued Ethelbald's work, conquering Kent, Sussex, Anglia and part of Wessex, and styling himself "King of All England." Offa also expanded Mercia by marrying his daughters to the kings of the West Saxons and Northumbria.

Unable to conquer Wales, he built Offa's Dyke, an enormous defensive earthwork that stretched about 160 miles, to protect against Welsh raids. It helped define the current Welsh border, and about half is still standing.

Offa strengthened international relations, and England began to emerge as a European power. The Frankish King Charlemagne admired Offa, and together they made important commercial agreements. Charlemagne's currency reform prompted changes to British coinage, making the silver penny the main monetary unit. Offa developed new laws, which influenced those of King Alfred, and founded numerous abbeys.

Shortly after his death, however, Mercian prosperity was undermined by rival Anglo-Saxon dynasties and Viking raids and invasion.

---

*The official date of rule begins upon the death of the monarch's predecessor, although the coronation may not take place the same year.

THE VIKINGS
800s

During the eighth to eleventh centuries hordes of Scandinavians spread out by land and sea across Europe, colonizing as far as Constantinople in the east and possibly even Newfoundland in the west. These Vikings (meaning "pirates"), or Norsemen, traded and raided their way across Europe. Famous for their maneuverable oceangoing longships, the sea warriors shocked contemporary chroniclers with the speed and ferocity of their attacks, and their readiness to sack churches and monasteries.

Britain at the time consisted of squabbling, disunited kingdoms, unequipped to mount a united front against invaders. In 865 a huge army of Norwegian and Danish Vikings seized Scottish and Irish coastal areas and most of northern and eastern England. Moves to the south and west, however, were successfully blocked by Alfred, king of Wessex, who negotiated the division of England between himself and the Danish king, the latter retaining the part to the north and east of Watling Street. This became known as the Danelaw, where Vikings settled as farmers, traders or craftsmen. (A later invasion, in 1013, put the whole of England under Viking rule for a brief period.)

Despite their popular image as terrifying barbarians, the Vikings brought to Britain their tradition of epic poetry, their art and their expertise as traders and in shipbuilding, and influenced the English language.

ALFRED THE GREAT
849–899 or 901; crowned 871

A truly great king, blessed with a vision beyond even his military prowess, Alfred headed an age of cultural achievement.

By 870 the Danes had taken East Anglia, Northumbria and Mercia (now in the Midlands) and attacked the kingdom of Wessex, pushing its Anglo-Saxon king, Alfred, back to Athelney, Somerset. He regrouped, successfully attacking the Viking force at Edington in 878, and retook London in 886. He then negotiated the division of England into two halves—the north and east under Danish rule (the Danelaw), the rest under Saxon control. He strengthened defenses by enlarging the navy and establishing fortified towns (*burhs*).

Alfred was, however, an intellectual as well as a military visionary, and a strong advocate of education. Viking attacks on monasteries had damaged British learning, and Latin had fallen out of use. To help repair these ravages, he personally translated history and philosophy books into English, including Pope Gregory's *Pastoral Care* and Bede's *Ecclesiastical History of the English People*. One of his most important acts was to unify Roman, Christian and Saxon law into a single code, the Doom book, the basis of modern British law.

Despite his legacy, Alfred is best known for an apocryphal story: During his campaigns against the Vikings, he supposedly sheltered in Somerset with a peasant woman, who left him looking after her baking. Distracted by battle plans, he let her griddle cakes burn. Initially furious, she quickly apologized once she learned her royal guest's identity!

ETHELRED THE UNREADY
968–1016; crowned 978

After a period of peace under Alfred's successors and the Danelaw, the Vikings conducted a campaign of destruction lasting from about 980 to 1014. The poorly advised king of England, Ethelred, decided to pay off, rather than resist, the attackers. This was known as Danegeld ("Dane gold," which was actually paid in silver) and to raise it he imposed crippling taxes on all his subjects. The Danes invaded anyway, demanding larger payments.

On Saint Brice's Day 1002, the panicking Ethelred ordered the massacre of Danes living in England, though his commands were probably not widely obeyed. That same year, in an attempt to appease the Danes and control their aggression, Ethelred married Emma of Normandy (a region of France that had been given over to the invading Norsemen). But Swein Forkbeard eventually conquered England, and in 1013 Ethelred was forced into exile in France. Forkbeard's death allowed him briefly to regain control, but he died shortly afterward.

The English love a nickname. *Ethel* meant noble or good and *rede* meant counsel or advice—"Ethelred" therefore meant "good counsel." But this was precisely what the king did not have, hence the tag *unrede* ("Unready"), "ill-advised." Given his inexperience and manipulative advisers, it seems unfair to condemn Ethelred completely. His reign brought economic prosperity, and his judicial reforms, carried out by Archbishop Wulfstan, were arguably the origin of the American grand jury.

KING CANUTE
c. 990–1035; crowned January 6, 1017

The deaths of both the Viking ruler, Swein Forkbeard, and King Ethelred in 1014 and 1016, triggered a vicious power struggle. Ethelred's heir, Edmund II "Ironside," resisted the expansion led by Forkbeard's son, Canute (Cnut), now king of Denmark, but he was eventually defeated in October 1016. To avoid future clashes, the two agreed to divide England, only for Edmund to die a month later and leave Canute in control.

Canute had a ruthless streak, ordering the murders of English rivals such as Edmund's brother, but his reign also brought prosperity and security from invaders. He married Ethelred's widow to secure the throne, and allowed England to retain most of its Anglo-Saxon government, though he divided the country into four earldoms. His Christianity and Church patronage (including a pilgrimage to Rome) helped win English support, and led to a famous story: Supposedly annoyed by sycophants telling him he was powerful enough to control the waves, he went to the seashore to prove that God alone had that power—and got very wet.

As well as England and Denmark, Canute took control of Norway and parts of Sweden, but this North Sea empire collapsed when he died in 1035. Details are sketchy, but it's known that two of his sons were rivals for the English throne. Harold Harefoot ruled for five years, in opposition to his half brother Hardecanute (Harthacanute), who took power when Harold died. His cruel, unsuccessful two-year rule ended, to general relief, with his death in 1042, returning England to Saxon rule under Edward the Confessor.

EDWARD THE CONFESSOR
c. 1004–1066; crowned April 3, 1043

The Anglo-Saxon King Edward the Confessor was the son of Ethelred the Unready, and a claimant to the throne after Hardecanute's death. His position was insecure—he returned from a twenty-five-year exile in Normandy to find many of his family's supporters replaced by Canute's—and his ability to establish control is a testament to his strength of character, contrary to popular depictions of a weak, unworldly king.

Edward's reign began over a prosperous England with strong European links—during his youth in Normandy, he had befriended many Norman nobles, including the future William the Conqueror. Half-Norman himself, there was broad Norman influence in his court, and this created resentment among the Saxon and Danish nobility, particularly the influential adviser Godwin, Earl of Wessex, whose daughter Edith he had married. Godwin was banished in 1051, though he was reinstated after returning the following year with a fleet. His son, Harold Godwinson, it was agreed, would inherit the throne, though it seems Edward might have already promised it to William first—and Edmund Ironside's grandson was the legitimate heir.

Edward's generosity to the poor and his piety earned him the title "Confessor." He built Westminster Abbey, where he is buried, and was responsible for creating its association with kingship; he was canonized in 1161.

Edward's childlessness and divided loyalties would change history. His death at the start of 1066, a "year of three kings," provoked a major succession crisis.

THE BATTLE OF HASTINGS
October 14, 1066

A rguably the most famous date in British history, 1066 was the last time anyone successfully invaded Britain.

The Normans maintained that King Edward the Confessor had promised the throne of England to William, Duke of Normandy. But Edward apparently had a dramatic change of heart on his deathbed when he declared Harold Godwinson, Earl of Wessex, his heir. William refused to accept this and decided to take his bequest by force.

King Harold II had just defeated a Norwegian army under Harald Hardrada at the Battle of Stamford Bridge in Yorkshire when William landed at Pevensey on the south coast. Harold's 5,000-strong army, footsore and exhausted, faced a Norman force of up to 15,000 infantry, archers and cavalry on a hill called Senlac (now Battle in honor of the area's history), near Hastings. At first Harold's men put up a ferocious defense with a wall of shields against which the Normans pitched themselves. Some of the invaders, given to believe William had been killed, started to retreat, but when the defending army broke ranks to pursue them, the Normans turned around and pushed forward, exploiting their enemies' disarray to the full.

Popularly believed to have been killed by an arrow in the eye (as depicted in the Bayeux Tapestry), although this is disputed, Harold was the last Anglo-Saxon king of England. His short but eventful reign over, his body was recovered and buried next to the battlefield. It was later moved to Waltham Abbey in Essex.

William of Normandy was crowned king of England at Westminster Abbey on Christmas Day 1066.

THE LATE MIDDLE AGES

THE TOWER OF LONDON
1070s–1100

Following his victory in 1066, William the Conqueror had a great stone tower built in the southeast corner of London's Roman city walls, serving as an observation post and stronghold against attack from unruly Londoners and possible invaders, as well as an assertion of the power of the new Norman monarch. Building work started during the mid-1070s and was completed by 1100. It was a huge edifice for its time, some ninety feet tall, and over the next 250 years or so was added to considerably, turning the single tower into the heart of a formidable fortress covering some eighteen acres. The original tower came to be called the White Tower because in 1240 Henry III had it whitewashed.

Over the centuries it has functioned as a royal residence, a fortress, a zoo, an arsenal, a prison (the earliest recorded inmate was Ranulf Flambard, Bishop of Durham, who escaped in 1101, and the most recent was Rudolf Hess, briefly in 1941), a place of execution (for example, Lady Jane Grey), and allegedly of murder (Henry VI, in 1471).

Today the Tower of London houses the Crown Jewels and a collection of arms and armor, as well as the ravens, who have each had one wing clipped to prevent them from flying away. According to a legend told to Charles II, if there were no ravens living there the White Tower would fall and great disaster to the nation would follow.

THE DOMESDAY BOOK
1086

The Domesday Book is the most important record of the social and economic life in medieval England. It was the result of a survey commissioned by William the Conqueror to record the resources and potential of England, and assess the revenue due to him. Property holders were asked details about who lived in the manor, their jobs, how much the land was worth, how many livestock, ploughs, mills and fishponds could be found, and so on. So probing was the investigation that it seemed to many as unchallengeable as the Last Judgment, which in the twelfth century led to its being named after Doomsday.

The survey covered most of the England of 1086, including a small part of what is now Wales, but excluding some areas north of the Tees. No records have been found for some major towns such as London and Winchester, either. Work appears to have stopped with the death of William in 1087, and what we are left with is the 475-page Little Domesday Book, containing detailed records of Essex, Suffolk and Norfolk, and the two-volume 413-page Great Domesday Book, which contains the edited-down accounts of most of the rest of England, written down by a single scribe on sheepskin parchment.

All in all, 268,984 individuals are mentioned, as well as 13,418 places, almost all of which still exist today, though many of their names have altered. Many manors were listed as "waste" due to the Norman army's destruction during the conquest.

THE FIRST CRUSADE
1095–1099

The Crusades were a series of religious wars waged over more than two centuries by much of Christendom to purge the dominant Muslims from the holy lands of the Middle East. The Seljuk Turks had conquered Jerusalem in 1076, and ruled over many Eastern Christians, but when they began harassing Christian pilgrims Pope Urban II took action. In 1095 he urged European Christians to liberate the Holy Land from the Muslims. The early Crusaders were disunited and without an obvious leader, and the First Crusade was as much a mass migration as an organized military campaign. Peter the Hermit, a priest, led a group of mostly civilian peasants and minor nobles, but, without military training and equipment, they were massacred in October 1096.

There followed a better organized military effort, a group of about 35,000, led mainly by European kings and nobles. These Crusaders traveled in disparate groups by various routes, with red crosses stitched to their chain mail. The knights waged a barbaric campaign against Muslims and Jews, including mass executions. In 1099 they reached Jerusalem and besieged it, eventually breaking through the walls and killing almost every inhabitant, regardless of religion. There, they founded the Christian Kingdom of Jerusalem; a small Christian enclave surrounded by Muslim kingdoms that, despite frequent attacks, lasted until 1187, when it was captured by Saladin.

European knights were encouraged to launch new Crusades, but meanwhile Arabic texts began to be studied by European scholars who developed an increasing appreciation of Muslim culture, eventually influencing the Renaissance.

HENRY II AND THE ANGEVIN EMPIRE
1133–1189; crowned 1154

William the Conquerer had been succeeded by two of his sons, William II and Henry I, though Henry's only son drowned in the wreck of "The White Ship" in 1120, leaving a question over succession. Henry's nephew, Stephen of Blois, gained the throne, only to fight a nineteen-year civil war ("The Anarchy") with Henry's daughter, the Empress Matilda (the rightful heir). Despite several military setbacks, Stephen clung on to power for the rest of his life, though he eventually recognized Matilda's son Henry as heir to the throne.

Upon Stephen's death in 1154, the new King Henry II became the most powerful ruler in Europe, presiding over the enormous Angevin Empire, having gained parts of northern France from his father Geoffrey of Anjou and much of southwestern France from his marriage to Eleanor of Aquitaine.

A man of great energy, Henry spent less than half his thirty-five-year reign in England, but was nonetheless an effective king. He consolidated Britain's uncertain borders, retaking Cumbria and Northumbria from the Scots, and was the first English king to visit Ireland and add it to his realm. He rectified much of the disorder that had developed under his predecessor Stephen, stamping down on corruption and beginning to replace trial by ordeal with jury courts, though for all that he is mainly remembered for his disagreement with Thomas à Becket.

Henry's relationship with his family was difficult, and the Angevin Empire fell apart under his ambitious and treacherous sons— the "Devil's Brood"—who rebelled against him in 1173. He died during peace negotiations with his son Richard, who succeeded him.

The family was called Plantagenet, it is thought after the sprig of *planta genista* (broom) that Geoffrey of Anjou adopted as a badge.

THE MURDER OF THOMAS À BECKET

December 29, 1170

Henry II's darkest hour was his clash with Thomas à Becket. Becket was originally Henry's loyal friend and chancellor, and for eight years he pursued an extravagant court lifestyle. But in 1162, Henry, irritated by Church interference, decided to manipulate the situation by making Becket Archbishop of Canterbury.

Becket's appointment, however, had a dramatic effect on him—he began to follow a pious and ascetic path, purging his sins with regular self-flagellation and wearing a hair shirt under his clothes. Now loyal to the Church, not Henry, Becket became committed to ecclesiastical independence, and angered Henry by resisting attempts to control him, fleeing to France in 1164. A tentative reconciliation six years later was wrecked when Becket punished bishops who had supported Henry. The king was furious, and an infamous outburst (one version of which is "Will no one rid me of this turbulent priest?") prompted four knights to take matters into their own hands. They rode to Canterbury and killed Becket in the cathedral, though whether their initial intent was murderous is uncertain.

Distraught and fearing excommunication, Henry walked in sackcloth to be flogged at Canterbury Cathedral. Becket's death was seen as martyrdom and Pope Alexander III used this opportunity to increase the Church's influence, knowing Henry wouldn't resist. Becket was canonized in 1173, and his tomb at Canterbury soon became a shrine and place of pilgrimage. His murder marked a turning point in relations between Church and State, and its legacy would endure until the Reformation.

RICHARD I "THE LIONHEART"
1157–1199; crowned September 3, 1189

Richard I became king after rebelling against his father, Henry II, and hounding him to an early grave. He joined Philip II of France on the Third Crusade, an attempt to recapture Jerusalem from Saladin's Muslim forces, which had taken it in 1187. He neglected his own country, spending only six months there in his entire reign, and was barely able to speak English—which did not stop him from imposing high taxes on his subjects to fund his adventures.

Richard reached the Holy Land in June 1191 and won major victories at Acre and Arsuf en route. He was ruthless in victory: After capturing Acre, Richard ordered the execution of 2,700 Muslim hostages. But disputes with Philip and Duke Leopold of Austria led them to desert Richard, and despite his remarkable achievements, Richard was unable to take Jerusalem. He agreed to a truce with Saladin in 1192.

Richard left for England, but was captured by Duke Leopold of Austria, who demanded a £100,000 ransom, an enormous sum at the time. That this could be raised from an already highly taxed nation is a testament to Richard's popularity, and the skill of the nobles who ruled in his stead.

In his absence, his brother John plotted against him with Philip II, but Richard returned in time to stop John from seizing the throne; however, he left for Normandy almost immediately to recover the French territories Philip had taken, and was killed by a crossbow bolt while besieging the Castle of Châlus.

KING JOHN
1166–1216; crowned 1199

An educated man, interested in the details of government and law, John nevertheless earned himself a reputation as treacherous, greedy and cruel—and disastrous in managing his subjects.

As the fourth and youngest son of Henry II, he was initially not given any land, hence his nickname, "Lackland." He conspired with his brothers against their father; then he conspired against his brothers. On the death of John's last surviving brother, Richard the Lionheart, Arthur, son of the third brother, claimed the throne—and conveniently disappeared, certainly murdered.

King from 1199, John angered the pope, who placed England under an interdict in 1208, excommunicating him in 1209. Neither action was permanent but church services were suspended, upsetting the people. John also lost vast territories in France to the French, earning a new nickname, "Softsword," and, to pay for the costly and unsuccessful attempts to regain them, imposed ever-higher taxes on his unhappy subjects. By 1215 his schemes to obtain money from his barons drove them to rebellion and they drew up a document, later known as Magna Carta, which they obliged him to put his seal to. This he did, but he did not adhere to its terms and soon the country was plunged into civil war.

As the embattled king traveled across Norfolk, his baggage train overturned in quicksands in the Wash. Its load included the Crown Jewels, never seen again. Soon after, the king fell ill, probably with dysentery (traditionally from consuming vast quantities of peaches and new cider), and he died in October 1216, leaving the crown to his nine-year-old son, Henry III.

MAGNA CARTA
June 15, 1215

Magna Carta (The Great Charter) is the most famous and most significant legal document in the history of democracy. Although it has come to carry symbolic weight where human liberties are at stake, it was not originally intended as a bill of rights. It was drawn up essentially to curb the powers of King John and to avoid a civil war. And it failed on both counts.

Among the most important of Magna Carta's sixty-three clauses were those guaranteeing freedom to the Church to make its own appointments; those restricting the feudal rights of the king; and those asserting the right of everyone to a fair trial and protection against illegal detention (a basis for *habeas corpus*), although many other clauses dealt with essentially minor grievances.

King John was not a popular monarch and the charter effectively listed the many faults in his ruling style. To keep his rebelling barons quiet and to buy time, he set his seal to the document. The new rules were supposed to be enforced by a council of twenty-five barons, and the terms of the charter were broadcast by public readings throughout the country. With Magna Carta, King John put everyone, not least himself and all future monarchs, within the rule of law. Neither king nor rebels adhered to its terms, however, and the country was soon in a state of civil war.

Nevertheless, it was reissued a number of times over the following years, and has remained an important symbol upholding English law and liberty.

EDWARD I AND THE RISE OF PARLIAMENT

1239–1307; ruled from 1272; crowned 1274

King Edward I, named Longshanks for his height of six feet two inches, was on the way home from the Crusades when his father Henry III died. Best known for his successful Welsh and Scottish campaigns, he arbitrated in a Scottish succession crisis in 1291, and appointed John Balliol king. But he demanded that Scotland recognize his own supremacy, and Balliol found himself answering to Westminster. When Edward demanded the Scots help him fight against France, the furious Scots sided with the French. In retaliation Edward began the conquest of Scotland, massacring the inhabitants of Berwick. Balliol was forced out, but William Wallace and Robert Bruce used powerful patriotic feeling to defend their political independence, while the English were never able to command the country.

Edward's wars required taxes, and hence frequent parliaments. These gradually came to play a major role in political life, and the 1295 Model Parliament defined the institution for centuries to come. Edward took an active interest in the machinery of his government, and it was during his reign that Parliament began to meet regularly for the first time.

Motivated partly by a need for money and partly by the anti-Semitism of the time (which already required Jews to wear yellow badges), Edward expelled England's Jews in 1290, seizing their property. They were allowed to return only in 1656.

SIR WILLIAM WALLACE
c. 1272–1305

William Wallace led a widespread revolt against the English overlordship of Scotland, and became a national hero. Scotland had become increasingly resentful of England's interference in its running, especially when it became clear that King Edward I, having seen John Balliol onto the Scottish throne in 1292, expected Balliol to provide funds and men for a planned invasion of France. In 1295, therefore, the Scots negotiated a treaty with France. In fury, the English invaded Scotland in 1296, sacked Berwick, defeated the Scots armies at Dunbar and took Balliol prisoner, forcing him to abdicate.

A full-blown rebellion began in May 1297 when William Wallace allegedly killed Sir William Haselrig, the English Sheriff of Lanark. He then went on to capture a number of English fortresses and on September 11, 1297, in the Battle of Stirling Bridge, his army, outnumbered as they were, defeated the English. The Scots capitalized on their success with bloody raids south of the border, and Wallace was elected to the office of guardian of the kingdom.

But in July 1298 a large English army defeated Wallace's forces at the Battle of Falkirk. Wallace was forced into hiding and then fled to France, returning a few years later only to be caught near Glasgow in 1305. He was brought to London, tried for treason— despite never having sworn allegiance to the English Crown—and hung, drawn and quartered.

ROBERT THE BRUCE
1274–1329

The Bruce family, one of the three most powerful noble families in Scotland alongside the Balliols and the Comyns, gave strategic support to King Edward I's invasion of Scotland in 1296, hoping to take Balliol's place on the throne, but their ambitions were thwarted when Edward decided to rule Scotland as an English province.

Robert the Bruce therefore chose to support the rebel William Wallace, leading revolts at Irvine and Ayr. After Falkirk was lost in 1298, Bruce, alongside his rival, John Comyn, was appointed a guardian of Scotland. In 1306 he killed Comyn and had himself crowned Robert I of Scotland. He was deposed by Edward I and fled, to come back a year later when Edward died and was succeeded by his weak son, Edward II. For years Robert waged guerrilla warfare against the English, which culminated in victory at the Battle of Bannockburn in June 1314. This confirmed Robert the Bruce's status as hero-king and strengthened his cause for an independent Scotland.

In 1320 a contingent of nobles wrote to Pope John XXII, in the "Declaration of Arbroath," to persuade him to proclaim Bruce as the rightful monarch. Papal recognition arrived in 1324, which reinforced Scotland's sense of national identity and resistance to English rule.

Robert renewed the Franco-Scottish alliance against the English but when, in 1327, Edward II was replaced by his son, Edward III, peace was made between Scotland and England—although the new king quickly reneged on his recognition of King Robert's independence.

THE HUNDRED YEARS WAR, PART 1
1337–1377

The Hundred Years War was an intermittent 116-year conflict between England and France. Its causes were rooted in long-standing Anglo-French tensions, largely related to the English Crown's possessions in France, particularly Gascony, in the southwest. A French succession crisis following the death of Charles IV in 1328 worsened the situation—Edward III of England's strong claim through his mother was denied and the throne given to his cousin Philip of Valois, who seized Gascony in 1337. In response, Edward invaded France. Although outnumbered and on unfamiliar ground, the English were better funded and equipped with longbows, which proved instrumental at the Battle of Crécy.

By 1340, the English navy had secured control of the Channel, capturing Calais in 1347. Meanwhile, Edward's eldest son, the "Black Prince," led a successful southwestern campaign, ending with the capture of the French king at Poitiers in 1356. In 1360 the French surrendered, handing over the southwest in return for Edward renouncing his claim to the throne.

Hostilities resumed in 1369, with the new French king, Charles V, driving the English back to the northwest. The French retook the Channel, and the Black Prince, a skillful and popular general, became ill and died in 1376.

In England, criticism of the king's high taxes and of his mistress Alice Perrers grew. Edward III died in 1377, a year after his son, as French forces encroached on England's coast.

THE BATTLE OF CRÉCY
August 26, 1346

The Battle of Crécy, in northern France, was the first decisive engagement of the Hundred Years War, and one which influenced the future of warfare.

Edward III's army had landed in Normandy, and was pursued by the French under Philip VI to the north bank of the Somme. Although heavily outnumbered, Edward's choice of location gave the English the advantage. Fighting took place on a hill where Edward could observe the action easily, with Welsh and English archers in position on either side of a core of infantry and dismounted knights, commanded by the sixteen-year-old Black Prince. Rain made the hill slippery, and the sun behind the English dazzled the French. The French cavalry repeatedly attempted to charge uphill, but were mown down by longbows, which were longer-ranged and faster-firing than the French crossbows. Thousands of French troops were killed, and Philip had to retreat.

The Battle of Crécy marked a shift in military methods. The feudal tradition of mounted knights, bound by strict codes, was challenged by the total defeat of the French nobility by peasant archers. Fighting on horseback began to decline, but the French repeated their mistake at Poitiers ten years later.

Edward III celebrated the victory by creating the Order of the Garter, one of Britain's highest honors that can be bestowed on only twenty-four members at one time, in addition to the reigning monarch and the Royal Knights.

THE BLACK DEATH
1348–1350

The Black Death was a gruesome plague pandemic that traumatized the populace from summer 1348 for over two years. Believed to have been transmitted to humans by fleas on infected rats, the disease killed tens of millions worldwide. The term "bubonic plague" refers only to the most common variant, which caused painful swellings on the neck, armpits or groin, turning black as the disease attacked the lymph nodes, often killing within a week. The septicemic variant caused blood poisoning, while the rarest and deadliest pneumonic form could kill in only two days by attacking the lungs. As churches ran out of consecrated land for graves, survivors resorted to mass burials in "plague pits." Settlements were left deserted and there were severe labor shortages. With no understanding of the disease, it is estimated that around half of Europe's population was killed.

In England, about one-third of the population died. The scale of death created major economic changes, many of them positive. Wealth was concentrated among the survivors, and social mobility increased. But there was widespread loss of confidence in the Church, which had conspicuously failed to explain or alleviate the disaster. It was widely seen as divine retribution for humanity's sins. Minorities, particularly Jews, were accused of engineering the plague, and violently persecuted.

By the end of 1350 the Black Death had mostly subsided, though sporadic outbreaks continued until the seventeenth century.

Recently, some scientists have suggested that the Black Death was caused not by plague, but by anthrax or a virus resembling Ebola.

THE PEASANTS' REVOLT
1381

In 1381 rural society was under strain; the Black Death had wiped out over a third of the workforce. In an attempt to control rising labor costs, a law had been brought in to restrict the surviving peasants' movements and cap their wages, but many workers still felt they had the right to command better conditions. Feudal serfdom was not only oppressive, but also forced the new landowning peasants to neglect their own plots. Added to this problem was a lack of confidence in the fourteen-year-old King Richard II's unpopular advisers. The introduction of a poll tax to pay for the Hundred Years War was the last straw.

In June 1381, Wat Tyler and John Ball emerged as leaders of a rebellion of laborers from all over the southeast, and marched on London to demand an end to feudalism. On their way they burnt tax records, stormed Marshalsea and Fleet prisons and destroyed property belonging to the king's advisers. Other protestors ransacked the Tower and murdered the Archbishop of Canterbury and the Lord Treasurer.

The young king met the rebels at Smithfield for negotiations. Tyler was stabbed to death by the Lord Mayor, creating uproar, but the king was able to calm the mob by promising to meet their demands—while his allies organized a militia. No sooner had the marchers dispersed than the king reneged on his promises and rounded up the leaders for execution. The offending poll tax, however, was revoked, and feudalism in England did not last much longer.

JOHN WYCLIFFE'S BIBLE AND THE LOLLARD MOVEMENT
1382–1395

John Wycliffe (*c.* 1320–1384), who taught philosophy at Oxford, was a theologian and religious reformer. He was strongly opposed to papal influence at court (and as this included levying tributes, King Edward III and his court were behind him), and criticized the Church for abusing its power, maintaining that the Bible, rather than the Church, was the supreme authority.

During 1378 Wycliffe and some Oxford associates defied the Church by deciding to translate the Bible from Latin into English, thus making it accessible to many more people. It appeared from about 1382 until roughly 1395, and became popular among Wycliffe's followers, many of whom could not understand Latin. The Church denounced it as inaccurate and tried to suppress it. It became an act of heresy to translate the Bible without papal approval (two centuries later William Tyndale translated the Bible from Greek and was strangled and burnt at the stake) and in 1382 Wycliffe was condemned as a heretic and expelled from Oxford. His supporters, who were given the derogatory name of Lollards, followed his teachings and saw to it that the Wycliffe Bible was widely distributed. They grew in number over the next twenty or so years but were severely persecuted, some burnt at the stake, so their following diminished. With Henry VIII's reign, the descendants of the Lollards began to join the growing forces of Protestantism.

THE HUNDRED YEARS WAR, PART 2
1377—1453

The French resurgence of the 1370s came to an abrupt halt in 1380 when Charles V died. His successor was still a child, and his court slid into factional disputes. Eventually Charles VI started to rule and a truce between England and France in 1389 began a twenty-six-year period of relative peace.

In 1392 Charles VI went mad and France fell into a state of civil war. The English under Henry V finally took advantage of this, and set out to regain French territories. Aided by the Duke of Burgundy, Henry reconquered Normandy, seizing Harfleur in 1415 and going on to Agincourt, where the English faced an army four times their size. Thanks to a great deal of mud, the heavy armor worn by the French and the English longbows, it was a triumphant victory for Henry.

Henry's domination seemed complete when he married the French king's daughter and was accepted as heir and regent of France in 1420. He died two years later, though, and was succeeded by his infant son, Henry VI. Saint Joan of Arc led a campaign against the English at the Siege of Orléans in 1429, but was captured and burned as a witch.

The tide turned when Burgundy switched sides in 1435, while Charles VII of France began military reforms, especially advances in artillery. The French proceeded to retake nearly all of France, bringing the war to an end in 1453; Calais alone remained English until 1558. With peace came improvements in the economic situations of both countries, and the development of stronger national identities. English superseded French entirely as England's spoken language.

GEOFFREY CHAUCER'S
THE CANTERBURY TALES
1387

Geoffrey Chaucer (1343–1400), known as the father of English literature, was born in London. Over the course of his life, he traveled widely and worked as a diplomat, courtier, lawyer and civil servant. His experiences influenced his writing, particularly his journeys to Italy where he appears to have been inspired by early Renaissance literature, especially Boccaccio and Dante Alighieri.

His first major work is believed to be *Book of the Duchess,* an allegory lamenting the death of Blanche, John of Gaunt's wife, in 1369. Other works include the poems the *Parlement of Foules* and *Troilus and Criseyde,* a major adaptation of a romance by Boccaccio.

Chaucer began his best-known work, *The Canterbury Tales,* in 1387. In it a group of pilgrims is traveling from London to Thomas à Becket's shrine in Canterbury, telling stories to pass the time. They are a diverse lot, from various occupations and backgrounds, clearly drawn from real life, and they paint a vibrant picture of contemporary English society in their vivid stories. Some, like the Miller's Tale, are bawdy, while others are serious or allegorical. There are 24 tales in total, but Chaucer had originally planned 120.

The Canterbury Tales is not the first work written in English, but it was important in popularizing English, rather than French or Latin, as England's literary language. The variation of style and tone in his work made Chaucer the greatest English poet of the period.

WILLIAM CAXTON
c. 1422–1492

The first printing press had been invented by the German Johann Gutenberg in about 1450, and the technology was brought to England by William Caxton. A successful diplomat and merchant, Caxton was governor of the English Nation of Merchant Adventurers from 1462 to 1470. By then he had been living for some twenty years in Bruges, before moving to Cologne.

He learned the art of printing in Cologne, returning to England in 1476 to establish the kingdom's first press, near Westminster Abbey. This development coincided with a period of peace and reconstruction under Edward IV, who patronized Caxton's press.

In England, as elsewhere, the printing press liberated reading and knowledge from Church control. Mass-produced books reduced the cost of learning, eroding the old monopolies on education and increasing social mobility. Writing played a greater part in national identity and intellectual life, and the adoption of printing led gradually to standardization of English spelling. (Caxton gave us certain unusual spellings such as "ghost," which derives its silent *h* from the Dutch/Flemish spelling.)

English had already superseded Latin and French as a spoken language, and it was now doing the same in literature, aided by Caxton's work as a translator—from Dutch as well as Latin and French. Lord Rivers' *Dictes and Sayinges of the Philosophers* was the first book printed in English. He printed about one hundred books, including Chaucer's *The Canterbury Tales* and Malory's *Le Morte d'Arthur*.

THE WARS OF THE ROSES
1455–1485

The Wars of the Roses were a lengthy power struggle between two branches of the royal family, both descended from Edward III: the Houses of York (with a white rose as its badge) and Lancaster (with its associations with the red rose, though this was later exaggerated in importance to give the conflict its name). The rivalry originated in the controversy created when Henry Bolingbroke (Henry IV), son of Edward III's third son, seized the throne in 1399 from his childless cousin Richard II.

By 1422, the Lancastrian Henry VI was king, but as he was weak and mentally unstable, Richard, Duke of York—who had a claim to the throne himself as a descendant of Edward's second son—had to rule briefly as Protector in 1454. Henry's return to sanity provoked war between the two houses, beginning in 1455 with a Yorkist victory at St. Albans, followed by another at Northampton. York was eventually killed at Wakefield, though his son avenged him at Towton in 1461 and seized the throne as Edward IV.

Edward ruled peacefully until he was deposed and exiled in 1470. Henry VI was briefly restored, but was imprisoned and murdered after Edward regained the crown in 1471. His young son Edward V succeeded him in 1483, but he and his brother mysteriously disappeared. Their uncle usurped the throne as Richard III, but was killed in 1485.

This turbulent period ended when the Lancastrian Henry Tudor, victorious at Bosworth, claimed the throne as Henry VII. His marriage to Elizabeth of York unified the warring houses, symbolized by the Tudor rose of both red and white.

RICHARD III
1450–1485; crowned July 6, 1483

Richard, youngest son of Richard Plantagenet, Duke of York, was the last Yorkist king of England. He had fought alongside his elder brother, Edward IV, notably at Barnet and Tewkesbury, and was named Protector for Edward's twelve-year-old son, Edward V, who became king after his father's death in April 1483.

Edward IV had provoked criticism by marrying Elizabeth Woodville, a widow and a commoner. After his death, on June 25, 1483, an assembly of nobles declared the marriage illegal and the young king and his brother illegitimate. The next day, Richard III seized the crown for himself, and the princes, who had been staying in the Tower, were never seen again. Their disappearance remains unsolved, but Richard's obvious gain led to rumors of his involvement, which lost him a lot of support.

Tudor historians described Richard as a cruel monster, deformed in body, mind and soul, as depicted in Shakespeare's *Richard III*. Modern research, however, tells a different story—he may have been calculating and ambitious, but these flaws were exaggerated, and references to his elegant dancing suggest his deformity was minor or nonexistent. His loyalty, bravery and piety have also been recently underlined.

Richard's reign survived a failed rising in 1483, but Henry Tudor's invasion in 1485 ended in Richard's death at the Battle of Bosworth. According to legend, Richard's crown was flung into a thornbush as he fell, where it was found and placed on Henry's head.

THE RENAISSANCE
c. 14th–17th centuries

The Renaissance (meaning "rebirth") was a revolution in European culture and society that heralded the modern age.

As explorers expanded the limits of geographic knowledge, European merchants traveled east to find luxury goods, learning new trading practices and Arabic numerals. World finance became more intricate, as a merchant class emerged, originally in the city-states of Italy, and capitalist economics developed.

Roman influences on European development had been largely forgotten, but the Byzantine empire, which retained Roman elements, influenced Italy through trade. Renewed interest in classical civilization defined Renaissance culture, particularly the arts, which flourished with commissions from merchant families. Architecture moved from Gothic to classically influenced designs, while artists developed greater realism, including the use of perspective.

The Renaissance was a time of humanist ideas, spread by the newly introduced printing press. New instruments and Middle Eastern science, including astronomy and algebra, allowed scientists like Galileo and Copernicus to make groundbreaking discoveries. "Renaissance men" such as Leonardo da Vinci excelled in many fields. Philosophical and scientific advances challenged Church authority and influenced the Reformation.

The Renaissance spread through Europe and first affected England during the late fourteenth and early fifteenth centuries, as writers such as Chaucer popularized English as a literary language. After the English Reformation, humanist literature experienced a resurgence often called the English Renaissance, Shakespeare's work being the best-known example.

TUDOR BRITAIN

HENRY VIII
1491–1547; crowned June 24, 1509

The reign of King Henry VIII began as a golden age in British history. Having inherited an overflowing treasury from his father and a legitimate claim to the throne from his mother, the young Henry was athletic, intelligent and religious, and a patron of the arts, particularly music and architecture. He disliked time-consuming administrative duties, and delegated to ministers such as Wolsey and Thomas Cromwell. However, he loved warfare, beating the French at Guinegate and the Scots at Flodden Field in 1513.

As his reign continued, Henry's temperament grew volatile. He was obsessed with producing a male heir, and famously married six times. His first wife, Catherine of Aragon—his elder brother Arthur's widow—produced only one surviving child, Mary. Henry claimed his marriage was blighted by God as a punishment for marrying his brother's wife, and after eighteen years he decided to annul it in order to wed Anne Boleyn, who would later bear Elizabeth. The pope's refusal to grant a divorce brought conflict with the Church, eventually leading to Henry's excommunication and the Reformation.

Suppressing political opposition, Henry beheaded anyone who displeased him, including many of his former ministers and his second wife, Anne Boleyn, and fifth wife, Catherine Howard. Between them were Jane Seymour—who died shortly after giving birth to his one male heir, Edward—and Anne of Cleves, whom he divorced after six months. Henry died in 1547, out of money and too fat to move unaided. His last wife, Catherine Parr, outlived him, and remarried.

THE REFORMATION
1529–1536

Henry VIII's roving eye and mission to father a son had led him into conflict with the pope and Europe's Catholic powers, although Henry in fact remained devoutly Catholic—the pope had earlier named him "Defender of the Faith" in gratitude for his public refutation of the ideas of the reformist cleric Martin Luther.

Henry secured his divorce by rejecting papal authority over the English Church, declaring himself Supreme Head of the Church in 1534, and ending the pope's control over a country that was still mainly Catholic. Anyone who actively disagreed was guilty of treason and executed. The Act of Supremacy marks the first time the salutation "Your Majesty" was used and heralded England's move toward becoming a legally self-sufficient empire. In 1549, Thomas Cranmer's Protestant Book of Common Prayer was completed and its use imposed on churches.

The break with Rome was just the beginning of the English Reformation, a wide-ranging movement that lasted for several decades. After a period of religious uncertainty, Elizabethan policies would crystallize a wide range of religious opinion into the Anglican Church Settlement.

But the English Reformation was part of a wider European movement that began with Luther in 1517. Strict dogma, financial extravagance and corruption by the Church hierarchy troubled European Catholics, and the Reformation was a reaction to those practices, with roots stretching back nearly 150 years to the work of reformists like John Wycliffe. The English Reformation was not simply a by-product of Henry's divorce.

THE DISSOLUTION OF THE MONASTERIES
1536–1541

After his divorce and the break with Rome, Henry VIII needed to reduce the Church's power in England, as well as find money to fund his fruitless and expensive wars against France and Scotland. His solution was to target the wealthy Catholic monasteries. In a five-year period, over eight hundred monasteries were dissolved, demolished for building materials, sold off to aspiring gentry or reclaimed as Anglican churches. Although monks and nuns were generally treated well, some who resisted were executed. Seizing property brought in less money than expected, so Henry also sold monastic lands to merchants and nobles, bringing new landowners to his side.

Although Henry bought support from the self-interested gentry, many Catholics, particularly in the North, were furious. A short-lived rising, the Pilgrimage of Grace, was dispersed by force in 1536–1537, though Henry did agree to some minor concessions. Although some clerics agreed with the principle of reform, they were aghast that the proceeds enriched the king rather than funding hospitals and schools to replace those that had been run by monasteries. The biggest losses were cultural—shrines were ransacked, altars looted and priceless manuscripts lost forever.

LADY JANE GREY, QUEEN FOR NINE DAYS
1536/7–1554

Lady Jane Grey had the shortest reign in British history, as Britain's first queen regnant. The young Jane was mistreated by her parents and found solace in books, which would lead her to become one of the most learned women of the time, a devout Protestant with a gift for languages. But she was manipulated by both her father, who attempted to marry her to Edward VI, and, later, after she married Lord Guildford Dudley, by her father-in-law, the Duke of Northumberland.

Sixteen-year-old Edward VI's health was failing and the subject of the succession was top of the agenda. Many wanted to keep the Catholic Princess Mary off the throne to uphold the Protestant Reformation. Northumberland, head of Edward's government, persuaded the king to overlook his half sisters, Mary and Elizabeth, claiming they were illegitimate despite the Catholic Mary being named the next in line in Henry VIII's will. Northumberland decided that Jane, granddaughter of Henry VII through his second daughter, was next in line. It was no coincidence that she was married to his son.

Edward VI died on July 6, 1553, and four days later Jane was proclaimed Queen by Northumberland. Mary, however, made an immediate counterclaim and quickly gained widespread support. Mary felt that Jane, if left alive, could be a focus for Protestant rebellion, so, on February 12, 1554, Jane, no more than seventeen years old, watched her husband's beheading at the Tower before being executed herself.

MARY I (BLOODY MARY)
1516–1558; crowned July 19, 1553

Henry VIII's only surviving child by his first wife, Catherine of Aragon, Princess Mary was stripped of her title, expelled from court and declared illegitimate on her parent's divorce. Her half sister, Elizabeth, suffered the same fate when her mother Anne Boleyn was executed, and it was not until 1544 that Mary and Elizabeth were restored to the line of succession, after their half brother Edward.

In 1547 Henry died, and the nine-year-old Edward VI became king under a protectorate, continuing Henry's religious policy and becoming increasingly Protestant. But the sickly boy king died in 1553, and after Lady Jane Grey's bid for the throne failed, Mary rode triumphantly into London to take the crown.

Mary initially enjoyed widespread support, largely due to sympathy for her earlier mistreatment. But her marriage to the future Philip II of Spain, in 1554, was unpopular with the English. Many feared the Spanish influence in Court, and Mary and Philip's fervent Catholicism was a threat, not least to those who had profited from the dissolution of the monasteries. Mary set about systematically repealing the Protestant reforms passed by her father and half brother, and revived laws against heresy. From 1555 she tyrannized leading Protestants in the Marian Persecutions, burning almost three hundred religious dissenters at the stake (including Thomas Cranmer) and earning her the nickname "Bloody Mary." In 1558, her unpopularity increased when her husband persuaded her into an unsuccessful war in France, and Calais, England's last continental possession, was lost.

Despite two phantom pregnancies, Mary died childless, in 1558, powerless to prevent the crown succeeding to her Protestant half sister, Elizabeth.

THE COUNTER-REFORMATION
1545–1563

The Reformation spurred the Catholic Church to make further reforms itself to counter those of the Protestants. In 1545 Pope Paul III convened the Council of Trent (in Trento, north Italy), which met over two years, and for two more two-year periods over the next eighteen years, with the aim of discussing the doctrinal and disciplinary questions raised by the Protestants, as well as tackling such contentious issues as the sale of indulgences (pardons), corruption in the priesthood, and other religious abuses. The basic structure and doctrines of the Catholic Church were upheld, but discipline and organization were much improved and the worldly excesses of the preceding years were curbed.

Pope Paul III also gave encouragement to new religious orders such as the Ursulines, the Capuchins and, especially, the Jesuits. These were a highly educated group under the leadership of Ignatius Loyola, dedicated to renewing genuine piety through preaching and instruction, and spreading their religion throughout the newly discovered parts of the world such as the Far East.

The effect of the so-called Counter-Reformation was felt largely in mainland Europe (and its colonies). By the end of Elizabeth's reign, Protestantism was the main religion of England and Scotland.

ELIZABETH I
1533–1603; crowned January 15, 1559

I *may not be a lion but I'm a lion's cub, and I have a lion's heart."* (Elizabeth I)

Elizabeth's forty-four-year reign began during a period of serious religious tension. The Protestant Church of England had been established under Henry VIII and Edward VI, but Mary I had brutally attempted to restore Catholicism. Elizabeth rejected Protestant and Catholic extremes in favor of a moderate Protestant Church that retained some Catholic traditions. She supported Protestantism abroad, angering Mary's widower Philip II of Spain—whose armada she then soundly defeated.

The queen governed wisely, appointing capable ministers, and she nurtured her public image carefully. Her success came with a price, however, and she was the subject of several assassination plots. An extensive network of spies was employed to maintain Elizabeth's hold on power and life.

Elizabeth promoted exploration and conquest by adventurers like Drake, Hawkins and Raleigh, and her reign also brought a literary resurgence that included the work of Shakespeare, Spenser and Marlowe.

For reasons that are still unclear, Elizabeth never married, and she came under considerable pressure over her succession. She was, however, able to use her lifelong status as the Virgin Queen as a diplomatic tool, manipulating enemies with marriage proposals, as well as claiming that she was married to England.

The Tudor period ended when she died, childless, in 1603, leaving her people with a firm sense of national identity, and her country as an increasingly powerful player on the world stage.

MARY, QUEEN OF SCOTS
1542–1587

Elizabeth's cousin, Mary Stuart, became Queen of Scots when she was six days old, and as a baby was betrothed to Henry VIII's son Edward as part of an Anglo-Scottish peace treaty. Her French mother was against the idea and hid Mary until her coronation at the age of nine months. The arrangement subsequently fell through, to the fury of Henry VIII who reacted with a series of Scottish raids called the Rough Wooing. For her safety Mary was brought up in France, marrying the future King Francis II in 1558. After his death, Mary returned to Scotland in 1561.

A moderate Catholic, she tolerated the growing number of Protestants in positions of power, including her half brother James Stewart. However, she went against his and Elizabeth's wishes by marrying her cousin, the English Catholic Lord Darnley, which strengthened the claim to the English throne of the son duly born to them, James. After marriage, Darnley became drunken, arrogant and controlling, having Mary's friend and private secretary David Rizzio murdered in 1566. Darnley himself subsequently died in February 1567 in a mysterious explosion. Both Mary and her future (third) husband, the Protestant Earl of Bothwell, were implicated. They married in May, which turned the Scottish nobles against her; civil war ensued. Mary's armies were defeated and she was forced to abdicate in favor of her baby son.

She eventually fled to England, seeking the mercy of Queen Elizabeth, whom she had never met. As Mary seemed something of a liability, Elizabeth kept her prisoner for nineteen years until she was beheaded after being implicated in one too many Catholic plots.

SIR FRANCIS DRAKE
1540–1596

Francis Drake, sailor, navigator and buccaneer, was a vital part of Elizabeth I's plan to reduce Spanish control of the New World. His contemporary reputation in England was heroic, but the Spanish knew him as a bloodthirsty pirate.

Drake began his nautical career with his cousin John Hawkins, together making a fortune in 1563 by abducting West Africans and selling them as slaves. This was a foundation of Britain's slave trade, and an enduring stain on Drake's modern-day reputation. Spanish settlers in the Caribbean were major clients, and Drake came into conflict with Spain over its regulation of foreign trade, attacking Spanish ships with the queen's tacit support.

In 1577, Elizabeth commissioned Drake to attack Spanish colonies on America's Pacific coast. By the time he arrived his fleet had been reduced from six to one flagship: the *Golden Hind*. After navigating the Straits of Magellan, at the tip of South America, he sailed north, establishing the port of Nova Albion somewhere on that coast. He looted millions of pounds' worth of Spanish treasure and spices, returning triumphant in 1580 via Indonesia and Africa, the first Englishman to circumnavigate the globe.

War with Spain broke out in 1585. Drake was second in command of the English fleet in resisting a Spanish invasion attempt, defeating the Spanish Armada conclusively. During an expedition in 1596, Drake died of dysentery off the coast of Panama.

THE SPANISH ARMADA
July–August 1588

The defeat of the Armada was the largest and most important engagement of the undeclared Anglo-Spanish War (1585–1604)—and the greatest English victory since Agincourt.

When Elizabeth I succeeded her half sister, Mary I, England swung back to Protestantism. Mary's Catholic faith had led to a close relationship with her cousin and husband Philip II of Spain, whose aim was to extend his rule over England. Following Mary's death, and after many years of increasing hostility, Philip decided to end Elizabeth's Protestant reign through the power of the Spanish Armada, a mighty fleet of large warships.

The English ships were smaller but their captains were clever and daring. Firstly, Sir Francis Drake made a surprise raid on the Spanish fleet at Cadiz, which set back the Spanish plans for a year. Then, in 1588, as the English lit beacons on coastal uplands to signal the arrival of the Armada, Drake and Lord Howard of Effingham pursued them with their fleet of smaller but more maneuverable ships. Drake once more caught them by surprise at Calais with his superior artillery, and scattered the Armada into the stormy North Sea. There they were harried up the east coast of England, and forced to round the northern tip of Scotland into the Atlantic via the west coast of Ireland, where much of their fleet was lost to shipwreck. Over 20,000 Spanish sailors lost their lives while the English lost no ships and only one hundred men. But it had been a narrow escape: The entire English fleet had been committed at once, and but for the weather would have been seriously endangered.

WILLIAM SHAKESPEARE
1564–1616

William Shakespeare is one of the world's greatest dramatists. He stands at the heart of English literature, his name recognized worldwide.

Not a great deal is known about Shakespeare's life. He was born in Stratford-upon-Avon, his father a glover and, later, alderman; his mother the daughter of a wealthy landowning farmer. He had a good education but left school at fourteen, marrying Anne Hathaway four years later. They had two daughters and a son, though the latter died aged eleven in 1596 ("Grief fills the room up of my absent child . . ."). It is thought that by then Shakespeare was living in London, his family staying in Stratford.

In London he embarked on a career as actor, poet and playwright. By 1594 he was a member of the Chamberlain's Men company of actors (the King's Men after Elizabeth's death), for which he wrote all his plays. Although dates of his works are uncertain, by 1592 he had written several plays—mostly comedies, as well as the Sonnets—dedicated to his patron, the Earl of Southampton.

Shakespeare's reputation grew as did the success of the Chamberlain's/King's Men, who were able to invest in the building of the Globe theater, which opened in 1599. Between 1590 and 1613 Shakespeare wrote poems, 154 sonnets and at least thirty-eight plays—comedies, histories, tragedies and the late tragicomedies. The great tragedies—*Hamlet*, *King Lear*, *Othello*, *Macbeth*—and plays such as *The Tempest* have a profundity and humanity rarely surpassed and conveyed in language that has moved audiences over the centuries. "Not of an age," his friend Ben Jonson wrote, "but for all time."

THE BRITISH EAST INDIA COMPANY
Established 1600

The exploration of the Age of Discovery brought the first international traders, among them the influential British merchants who founded the British East India Company in 1600. Elizabeth I, aiming to reduce Dutch control of the Asian spice trade, granted them a monopoly on English trade in the East Indies. However, lasting influence came only when the Company secured the favor of India's Mughal rulers. This created numerous trading opportunities, particularly in the textiles industry.

Anglo-Indian trade was stable until the first half of the eighteenth century, when the Mughal Empire disintegrated into smaller states and France established itself as a rival power in India. Indian states began taking sides and the Company expanded militarily, with Robert Clive taking the south during the Seven Years War (1756–1763). His great victory was at the Battle of Plassey in 1757, which allowed him to conquer Bengal. Although initially laissez-faire, the Company's policy grew imperialist toward the end of the century, and it took over a section of Asia stretching from Afghanistan to Burma. The reaction of the British government to the Indian Mutiny ended Company rule in 1858.

Meanwhile, the Company was growing opium in Bengal and illegally importing it into China, beginning in 1781. Attempts in the late 1830s by Chinese authorities to end smuggling created tension between China and Britain, leading to the First Opium War (1839–1842).

The Company was dissolved on January 1, 1874.

STUART
BRITAIN

JAMES VI OF SCOTLAND AND I OF ENGLAND

1566–1625; crowned James I July 29, 1603

James VI of Scotland was the only son of the Roman Catholic Mary, Queen of Scots, and became king of Scotland at the age of one, when his mother abdicated and fled to England and imprisonment, leaving her son behind in Stirling Castle. He was brought up a Protestant, and married Anne of Denmark, a Lutheran. He supported Elizabeth I against Catholic France and Spain, and barely complained when she had his mother executed (a "miserable accident," Elizabeth called it), so on the queen's death in 1603 he was welcomed as her heir.

He had been King James VI of Scotland for thirty-six years; now he became James I of England as well, and became head of the Church of England. He lacked Elizabeth's sophistication and poise, but his intellect and firm belief in the divine right of kings overcame that disadvantage. He tried, not very successfully, to achieve religious peace across Europe—even attempting to appease Spain by having Sir Walter Raleigh, still a national hero, executed, ostensibly for attacking a Spanish colony in Guiana—but at home his reign was generally a good one, even though his adherence to the royal prerogative led to quarrels with his parliaments, who thought differently.

He was obsessively antiwitchcraft (Shakespeare's witches in *Macbeth* were partly for his benefit), and antismoking, writing of "this vile custom of tobacco taking . . . dangerous to the lungs." His characteristic blend of ineptitude and cleverness gave him the nickname, "The Wisest Fool in Christendom."

THE GUNPOWDER PLOT
November 5, 1605

If the Gunpowder Plot, planned for the State Opening on November 5, 1605, had gone according to plan, the Houses of Parliament would have blown up spectacularly and been reduced to rubble; Westminster Abbey would probably have been flattened; and King James I and his largely Protestant government and Parliament would have been wiped out.

The ultimate aim was to restore civic rights to Roman Catholics. Monarch and Parliament out of the way, the plotters, a group of Catholic extremists, planned to place James's nine-year-old daughter on the throne as Catholic puppet monarch.

On the night of November 4–5, Guy Fawkes, their explosives expert, was waiting by the thirty-six barrels of gunpowder they had smuggled underneath the Houses of Parliament, ready to light the fuse. But an enigmatic warning sent to a Catholic peer not to attend Parliament had aroused suspicion and guards were sent to check the cellars. Fawkes was arrested and tortured until he named his coconspirators, who were duly rounded up and tried. To no avail, most pleaded not guilty: They were sentenced to be hung, drawn and quartered. As he was being hanged, Fawkes jumped off the gallows, breaking his neck before his executioners could implement the next two grim steps.

Unsurprisingly the Catholic cause suffered a severe setback: Emancipation took another two hundred years. To celebrate his survival, King James declared that his subjects should light great bonfires every 5th of November.

THE KING JAMES BIBLE
1611

Until the fourteenth century there was no complete English translation of the Bible. The first full English Bible was Wycliffe's in 1382. In 1525 William Tyndale began his translation; although he did not complete it, his was the first printed English Bible, and formed the basis for Myles Coverdale's authorized "Great Bible" in 1539, revised as the Bishops' Bible in 1568. When James I succeeded Elizabeth in 1604, both the Coverdale versions were in use, as were a number of others, including the Roman Catholic Douai and the Calvinist Geneva Bible.

James's reign saw the rise of radical Protestants, or Puritans, who promoted thrift, education and private enterprise. They wanted to simplify, or purify, church rituals and to limit the powers of bishops—who propped up royal authority—and as they were well represented in Parliament, the king was anxious to appease them. So when they voiced several reservations about the current translations of the Bible, he saw his chance and ordered a new version.

Forty-seven carefully selected scholars set to work, and in 1611 the completed King James Bible, still owing much to Tyndale, was issued. It is still regarded as the finest English-language version ever produced, widely praised for the beauty and simplicity of its style.

THE PILGRIM FATHERS AND THE *MAYFLOWER*
1620

The Pilgrim Fathers were a group of about one hundred people who fled religious persecution in England to colonize what is now New England in America.

Although it was hoped that the accession of James I in 1603 would bring religious tolerance, Separatist Puritans were still persecuted, and in 1607 some thirty Separatists in Scrooby, Nottinghamshire, fled to the Netherlands, settling ultimately in Leiden.

They had difficulty preserving their culture, however, and, attracted by the fishing and missionary work available in America, they negotiated a land patent with the London Virginia Company, which had established the first English colony at Jamestown in 1607. They joined other would-be settlers in Plymouth, Devon, and, on September 16, 1620, set sail in the 180-ton *Mayflower*.

The ship was overcrowded and too small for an ocean crossing, and many settlers died of disease. Damaged and blown off course, the *Mayflower* arrived, on November 21, at Cape Cod—well outside its destination of the Virginia colony. On December 21, forty-one of the surviving travelers drew up the Mayflower Compact of government for the colony, founding the town of Plymouth, in modern-day Massachusetts. The first winter was harsh, but the aid of Native Americans, and the security afforded by military leader Myles Standish, allowed them to survive and expand. In 1630, more English Puritans arrived and the Massachusetts Bay Colony was established. Boston became a major port and a wave of migration to the New World began.

THE FOUNDING OF NEW YORK
1626

In 1524, Giovanni da Verrazano, an Italian working for the French, had discovered a bay on America's east coast, naming it Nouvelle Angoulême. English explorer Henry Hudson, working for the Dutch East India Company, found the bay's largest island—Manhattan—in 1609, before sailing up the river now named after him. Manhattan's southern tip was the site of a Dutch fur-trading colony, New Amsterdam, founded in 1625. The following year, the island was purchased from its Native American inhabitants (supposedly for twenty-four dollars' worth of beads, which now seems unlikely).

In 1664, amid mounting Anglo-Dutch tensions over trade, English troops annexed the area unresisted, giving it the name New York after their commander, the Duke of York (later King James II). Such incursions sparked the Second Anglo-Dutch War, but the English were allowed to keep the city when the war ended. In 1673, during the Third Anglo-Dutch War, the Dutch retook the city, briefly renaming it New Orange. The peace terms of the war returned the city to English control the following year, and it continued to grow in prosperity.

CHARLES I
1600–1649; crowned February 2, 1626

Charles I inherited from his father, James I, an absolute belief in the divine right of kings, but was far less willing to listen to his subjects (and was considerably less intelligent!). He was disliked for his French Catholic wife, Henrietta Maria, and his support for Arminianism, a religious movement with pseudo-Catholic elements.

Charles needed money for a war in Spain, but Parliament, unhappy with military mismanagement, repeatedly refused to grant the funds that might have brought success. Charles dismissed it in 1629, beginning an autocratic eleven-year Personal Rule during which he constantly turned to obscure and unpopular taxes.

Charles was equally insensitive to his responsibilities in Scotland, and when he tried to impose a new Arminian prayer book on the Presbyterian Scots in 1637, widespread rioting ensued, eventually leading to a revolution and a Scottish invasion. Charles had to summon Parliament twice in 1640 to resolve this problem, but the first (the Short Parliament) refused to grant money and was dismissed after three weeks. Charles resorted to selling honors and pawning some of the Crown Jewels, managing to raise an army only to see it defeated at Newburn.

His resources now completely exhausted, he had to call Parliament again. But this only brought further disagreement, with the MPs refusing to allow the Parliament to be dissolved unless they agreed (this "Long Parliament" lasted in some form until 1660). A rebellion in Ireland required Charles to raise more troops, but Parliament, fearing such an army would be used against it, refused and demanded further reforms. Charles's decision to arrest troublesome MPs in 1642 led to the Civil Wars—and his eventual execution.

THE CIVIL WARS
1642–1649

For nearly seven years, Stuart Britain was torn apart by civil war. Religious and political tensions erupted in a power struggle between Royalists (Cavaliers) and Parliamentarians (Roundheads).

Charles I faced growing dissent from Parliament, which he attempted to suppress by force, provoking more hostility. Over the summer of 1642, Britain was divided, with the north, the west and Wales siding with the king; and the southeast (with its greater financial resources) with Parliament. In August, Charles raised his standard at Nottingham and war began.

The first battle, at Edgehill, was largely inconclusive, and the next year was occupied mainly in minor engagements, with Royalists making gains in the north and west. In 1643, the Earl of Essex won Parliament's first decisive victories at Gloucester and Newbury. The following year, Parliament, with the aid of the Scots, gained control of the north at the Battle of Marston Moor, where the cavalry tactics of Oliver Cromwell proved decisive.

With his forces restructured into the disciplined New Model Army, Cromwell achieved victory at Naseby and at Langport in 1645, and Charles surrendered to the Scots. But, with Parliament's attentions directed elsewhere, he negotiated Church reform with Scotland. The Second Civil War followed as Scotland switched sides and Royalist uprisings broke out. Parliament retained control, defeating the Scots at Preston.

The king was found guilty of treason—the first time a king had been tried in court—and was beheaded in 1649. Until the end he protested that the court had no jurisdiction over him as his authority came directly from God.

OLIVER CROMWELL AND THE COMMONWEALTH
1649–1658

Country gentleman, MP, soldier and brilliant strategist, Oliver Cromwell (1599–1658) rose to prominence during the Civil Wars. From 1649 to 1660 England was without a monarch, ruled by Parliament as the Commonwealth from 1649, then under Cromwell's personal rule as Lord Protector from 1653 until his death.

Cromwell expanded British trade internationally, but his most controversial policy was closer to home—he is still hated in Ireland (which he conquered in 1649–1650, contracting malaria on the way) for the massacres at Drogheda and Wexford. He then quelled a Royalist rebellion in Scotland, and an uneasy peace prevailed.

However, these campaigns detracted from his role in politics and the Rump Parliament (so called after it had been purged of Royalists, moderates and much of the aristocracy) descended into infighting. The Barebone's Parliament (named for an MP who gloried in the name Praise-God Barebone) was nominated, not elected, and was similarly unsuccessful. Cromwell adopted some aspects of monarchy toward the end of his reign, and in 1657, was offered the crown. He agonized for weeks before declining it—but his installation as Lord Protector resembled a coronation, with an ermine-lined robe, sword and scepter.

Although he promoted evangelical Puritanism, Cromwell was comparatively tolerant of other religions, and indeed encouraged Jews, banished by Edward I, to return to England.

In 1658, Cromwell died from a combination of malaria and kidney infection. His son Richard succeeded him, but soon resigned; the Rump returned and Charles II was restored in 1660.

THE RESTORATION OF THE MONARCHY
1660–1685

After Cromwell's death in 1658, he was succeeded by his son Richard, but his attempts to reconcile the growing enmity between Parliamentarians and the army were unsuccessful, and after eight months he was forced to abdicate. A group of MPs and officers, led by General George Monck, felt the only solution was to offer Charles I's son, also named Charles, the throne.

On his thirtieth birthday in 1660, King Charles II returned from several years of exile on the continent to reclaim the crown. There was minimal recrimination toward those who had deposed his father: Charles executed only nine Republicans and accepted parliamentary limits on his power. Within Parliament, the Civil War factions evolved into forerunners of modern parties—the Tories (Royalists with court links and High Church Anglicans) and the Whigs (parliamentarian landowners, Low Church dissenters and the merchant interest).

The Restoration brought a revival of the gaiety of the Elizabethan age in the form of dancing, sport and theater, particularly the risqué Restoration comedies. However, Charles's hedonism led him to rule lazily, often postponing policy decisions. Defeat in a trade war with the Dutch was blamed on his indifference, while his many mistresses were unpopular, particularly as tax money went toward their upkeep—although Nell Gwynne, the prominent actress, won friends with her frank claim that she was, at least, the "*English* whore."

Charles was not without political intelligence, promoting tolerance of Catholicism (allying with Catholic France against the Dutch, and ultimately converting on his deathbed) and successfully relegitimizing the monarchy.

THE GREAT PLAGUE AND THE GREAT FIRE OF LONDON
1665 and 1666

In the mid-seventeenth century, London suffered two major disasters in as many years, the second ending the first. From 1665, many thousands of people (possibly a fifth of London's population) were killed by a bubonic plague outbreak, exacerbated by heat, poor sanitation and slum housing.

Meanwhile, the summer heat of 1666 had already caused several fires. In September, fire broke out at a Pudding Lane bakery and spread quickly, fanned by an east wind and fueled by London's timber construction. The Lord Mayor failed to contain it quickly and it took four days to burn out, mostly obliterating the old city. Roughly 13,000 homes were destroyed, leaving 100,000 homeless but comparatively few dead. On the positive side, the fire destroyed many of the unhygienic slums, killing the rats and fleas that spread the plague.

Coming so soon after the Restoration, republicans, Catholics and foreigners were suspected in the hysterical hunt for a culprit. A French watchmaker, Robert Hubert, was hanged after he "confessed," despite his obvious mental disability.

Rebuilding proceeded along a less unsanitary version of the old plan, avoiding the expense of various grandiose proposals and allowing Londoners to retain their previous patches of land. The architect Sir Christopher Wren was hired to rebuild the city's churches, most famously St. Paul's Cathedral, and the 197-foot monument to the fire. Until 1831, that landmark bore a plaque blaming "the treachery and malice of the Popish faction." The Baker's Company officially apologized for the fire in 1986.

TITUS OATES AND THE POPISH PLOT
1678

In the aftermath of the Great Fire of London, conspiracy theories flourished in a climate of anti-Catholic hysteria. Titus Oates (1649–1705), an unsavory Baptist cleric, alleged drunkard and sodomite, returned from a period as a spy in France, claiming to have discovered a Catholic conspiracy to murder Charles II and replace him with his Catholic brother, James. Parliament took this claim seriously, and many innocent Catholics were arrested or killed as anti-Catholic hysteria grew (and an investigating magistrate was found dead in mysterious circumstances). Oates warned of further arson attacks on London, and there were even fears of a second Gunpowder Plot.

The plot led to the Exclusion Bill, a Whig attempt to prevent James's succession that provoked a lengthy crisis between 1678 and 1681 and destabilized Charles's authority, though the Exclusionists were divided over who should take James's place. Eventually, investigators realized the plot was entirely fictitious, and Oates was arrested, convicted of sedition, fined and thrown into prison. When James succeeded Charles II in 1685, he took revenge by having Oates retried. Oates was convicted of perjury, flogged, put in a pillory—to be pelted with all manner of unpleasant objects—and sentenced to life imprisonment. He was released in 1688 with the Glorious Revolution but never pardoned.

JAMES II, THE LAST CATHOLIC KING
1633–1701; crowned 1685, deposed 1688

Charles II had sons by various mistresses, but no legitimate heirs. The crown therefore passed to his brother, the devoutly Catholic James. Like his father but unlike his predecessor, James was a firm believer in the divine right of kings and unwilling to negotiate with Parliament.

James II granted greater freedom to Catholics, but did so without Charles's diplomacy, overriding Parliament's vocal objections and alienating many supporters in doing so. "Popery" was still feared by many, especially with news of French persecution of Protestant Huguenots. This led to Protestant uprisings such as the Monmouth Rebellion, which James II dealt with by force.

James's fate was sealed by the birth of a healthy male heir, James, in 1688 to his Catholic second wife, Mary of Modena (James also had two Protestant daughters by his first wife, Mary and Anne, both of whom went on to rule). The prospect of a continuing Catholic monarchy prompted a group of notable Protestants—the "Immortal Seven"—to take action. They invited James's daughter, Mary, and her husband, William of Orange, to come from the Netherlands and overthrow the king. As William landed at Torbay, James fled in panic to France, where his son, "The Old Pretender," later declared himself king in exile. Meanwhile, Parliament was able to declare that James had in effect abdicated, and William III and Mary II were proclaimed joint sovereigns of England and Scotland in 1689.

THE MONMOUTH OR PITCHFORK REBELLION
1685

Charles II's most charismatic, and firstborn, illegitimate son was James Scott, Duke of Monmouth, who claimed the throne, arguing (without producing any evidence) that the king had secretly married his mother. Monmouth and the king's brother James quarreled before Charles's death over the succession. Once the Rye House Plot, a scheme to murder both Charles II and James, was uncovered, Monmouth—who was implicated—fled to the Netherlands with his Protestant entourage.

As James II was crowned, Monmouth and his allies decided that only an invasion would save England from Catholic dominance. Monmouth headed for the strongly Protestant southwest, with a fleet of just three ships. James sent a small force led by the Duke of Marlborough.

When Monmouth landed, he had too few supporters to march on London, so he headed for Somerset, collecting an army of about 6,000 laborers, armed with pitchforks. He proclaimed himself king in Taunton, but after a few minor skirmishes the Navy captured his fleet.

The rebels were counting on a rebellion in Scotland that failed to materialize, and Marlborough pushed them back to Sedgemoor. Monmouth's attempted surprise attack was compromised by a premature musket shot, and the inexperienced rebels were quickly defeated. Monmouth fled, but was quickly caught, sent to the Tower, and beheaded. The trials of his followers were known as the Bloody Assizes, where 320 men were hanged and 800 deported to the West Indies.

THE GLORIOUS REVOLUTION
1688

In response to the entreaties of the Immortal Seven, William of Orange (1650–1702) invaded England with an enormous Dutch fleet, and was welcomed in Devon with banners celebrating "English liberties and the Protestant religion."

Although the Glorious Revolution was largely bloodless in England, fierce fighting occurred in Scotland and Ireland, where the deposed James unsuccessfully attempted to harness local sympathies and regain the crown from his daughter and son-in-law. Jacobite (pro-James) risings in Scotland and England continued sporadically for decades.

William III managed to persuade Parliament to agree to let him reign jointly with his wife Mary II, and they were crowned in February 1689. Parliament affirmed its authority with the Bill of Rights, a document that influenced later constitutional law worldwide. The Bill prohibited "cruel and unusual punishment" and, together with the 1694 Triennial Act, established regular Parliaments. Catholics were barred from the throne in the Act of Settlement, allowing the will of the nation to override hereditary right of succession, and William's attempts to secure toleration of Catholicism (a gesture to Catholic allies in Europe) were swiftly stopped by Parliament, although greater freedom was extended to Nonconformist Protestants in the 1689 Act of Toleration.

William III died in 1702 after his horse stumbled on a molehill, and Jacobites toasted "the little gentleman in black velvet" who had brought down their enemy. William and Mary, who had died in 1694, were childless, so the throne went to Mary's sister Anne (1665–1714) who, as a Protestant, had reluctantly deserted her father James II.

THE UNION OF ENGLAND AND SCOTLAND
The Act of Union, May 1, 1707

The political union of England and Scotland had its roots in the personal union of the crowns under James VI/I. Anglo-Scottish tensions had risen during the Civil Wars, and the 1690s brought turmoil in the wake of the Glorious Revolution, culminating in the Massacre of Glencoe.

To enhance its failing economy, weakened by English trade wars and a series of bad harvests, Scotland attempted to establish a colony at Darien, Panama, in 1698. Most of the colonists died, and Scotland suffered crippling financial losses after England withdrew support. Despite widespread fury at this betrayal, it seemed union might now be an economic necessity. In addition, it would secure William III's position in Scotland.

In 1701, the Act of Settlement, Parliament's legislation on succession in both countries, was passed without consulting the Scots, who then threatened to side with France and the Jacobites. London produced an ultimatum—the 1705 Alien Act—threatening harsh trade and property restrictions unless Scotland discussed union by Christmas Day.

After protracted negotiations, Scotland agreed to unite with England and Wales into Great Britain, retaining its separate legal and religious systems (and gaining compensation for the disastrous attempt to colonize Darien) but giving up political and economic independence. Even today, the Union remains controversial in Scotland, and many Scots favor repealing the Act.

MARLBOROUGH'S VICTORIES
John Churchill, First Duke of Marlborough 1650–1722

Marlborough's military career spanned five reigns. As a page to James, Duke of York (the future King James II), he picked up his master's passion for warfare. He became an increasingly important soldier and diplomat, playing a key role in defeating the Monmouth Rebellion.

However, like many of the king's supporters, he opposed James's religious policy, and defected to William. Relations with William and Mary were problematic—Marlborough fell from grace and was briefly imprisoned. However, his wife Sarah was a close friend of Queen Anne, and his career regained momentum during her reign.

In 1701, an illegal attempt by Louis XIV to secure the Spanish throne led to the War of Spanish Succession, as several countries united against French dominance. Marlborough saved Vienna at the Battle of Blenheim in 1704, France's first major defeat in forty years. Further victories at Ramillies, Oudenarde and Malplaquet drove France from the Netherlands. The 1713 Treaty of Utrecht ended the war, granting Britain large areas of French territory in what is now Canada, and Gibraltar and Minorca from Spain. As French power declined, the seeds for the British Empire were sown.

To commemorate his greatest victory, Anne gave Marlborough the old royal hunting estate at Woodstock, in Oxfordshire, and commissioned the architect Vanbrugh to design Blenheim Palace for him. After the war, Marlborough worked mainly in politics, with mixed results, until his death in 1722.

GEORGIAN BRITAIN

GEORGE I
1660–1727; crowned October 20, 1714

George Louis, Elector of Hanover, became king after the death of Queen Anne, who, despite having borne nineteen children, had no surviving heirs. George beat fifty-seven relatives with stronger claims by hereditary right, benefiting from the 1701 Act of Settlement, which barred Catholics from the throne. He was not a popular king; he spoke no English and preferred to spend time in Hanover, delegating domestic administration to ministers. Unlike Anne, George supported the Whigs, whom he appointed to all major positions. His lack of interest in domestic affairs meant his cabinet, left to run the country, grew increasingly powerful.

He did, however, take a keen interest in foreign policy, allying with France and the Netherlands against Spain in 1717. But the War of Spanish Succession left Britain $76 million in the red, so to fund government debt, shares were sold in the South Sea Company, a monopoly set up to trade with South America. At first, speculation drove shares to rocket in value. But a number of directors sold out, and the stock crashed in 1720, bankrupting thousands of private investors. Accusations of ministerial corruption were everywhere, and public anger led to a failed Jacobite conspiracy involving Tory MPs.

The bursting of the "South Sea Bubble" resulted in the Bank of England taking charge of the national economy. Robert Walpole's work in managing the crisis led to his appointment as First Lord of the Treasury, and as the clear leader of the ministry, the first "prime minister" (although this was only used as a term of abuse at the time).

PENAL COLONIES IN AMERICA AND AUSTRALIA
c. 1718–1868

In the early 1700s, growing revulsion at public executions and concern over public order led to the Transportation Act of 1718, which allowed courts to sentence convicts to seven years in America to work on roads, at construction sites and down mines, or as indentured servants. Fifty thousand British convicts were deported to America, including Scottish and Irish prisoners of war. Conditions were harsh, and many died from hunger, from disease or in desperate attempts to escape.

But American independence stopped this, and with industrialization causing rising crime and prison overcrowding at home, the government turned to Australia.

New South Wales, the largest Australian penal colony, was established in 1788, soon followed by others; 150,000 were exiled to Australia over the next eighty years. The convicts, mostly nonviolent petty criminals, trade unionists and supporters of Irish independence, were forced to work long hours with little food and harsh corporal punishment. Nonetheless, some intentionally committed crimes in England in the hopes of a new life in Australia.

Over the first half of the nineteenth century, public opinion in the colonies began to turn against transportation, as unpaid convict labor took work from paid laborers and increased crime rates. The discovery of gold in Australia in 1851 prompted a massive influx of free immigrants, who largely shared these views. Penal transportation tailed off, ending completely in 1868.

BONNIE PRINCE CHARLIE
Prince Charles Edward Stuart, 1720–1788

The House of Stuart had for several years been waging an ill-fated claim to the British throne after James II had been unseated in 1688. In 1744, his son James, "The Old Pretender," secured support from France for an invasion. That year, bad weather and British defenses made it impossible, but, in July 1745, "The Young Pretender," Charles Edward Stuart, grandson of James II, landed in Scotland and raised an army of mainly Scottish Highland clans.

The British military was too overstretched by the French war to defend Scotland, and the Jacobites invaded it with ease. They reached as far south as Derby, 127 miles from London (where George II had his bags packed, ready to flee), but soon found themselves spread too thinly, and were forced to retreat northward. A Hanoverian army under the Duke of Cumberland pursued them, only to be defeated at Falkirk. But at Culloden Moor the prince's command proved disastrous. He positioned his troops on open ground, where they were bombarded by artillery, before sending them charging into Cumberland's guns. It was the last pitched battle on British soil, and all hopes of a Jacobite restoration were lost as Cumberland embarked on a brutal campaign of repression against remaining Jacobites, earning the nickname "Butcher."

Charles was forced to escape to the Isle of Skye and then to France, disguised as a maid. He secretly returned to London in 1750, unsuccessfully trying to raise support for further rebellions. In 1788, he died a lonely alcoholic in Rome.

ANNUS MIRABILIS, THE YEAR OF VICTORIES
1759

The Seven Years War (1756–1763) was a worldwide land and naval conflict between imperial powers in America, Europe and Asia. Britain and France vied for colonial supremacy, allying with the old enemies Prussia and Austria, respectively. Although the early years went badly for Britain (except in India), Anglo-French battles culminated in 1759 with several spectacular British victories.

William Pitt (the Elder), then secretary of state, had been directing the war for two years. He invested in more troops and appointed young, ambitious commanders, a policy that paid off with victory at the Battle of Minden, Germany, in August. Pitt also supported Prussia financially, aiding its defense against hostile neighbors. The strengthened navy secured victories in the West Indies and West Africa and blocked the French from bringing further troops into America. General Wolfe heroically conquered Quebec in September, but the naval victory at Quiberon Bay off Brittany was equally important, crippling the French fleet and rounding off a spectacular year.

Pitt's dynamic leadership is often credited with ushering in the Age of Empire. The use of Scottish regiments, after the fall of Jacobitism, consolidated national unity. The 1763 Treaty of Paris ended the war and enlarged the British Empire, which now stretched from Canada to East India.

GEORGE III, PATRIOT KING
1738–1820; crowned September 22, 1761

George III was the grandson of George II, his father having died in 1751. He was the first Hanoverian monarch born and educated in Britain, and made the most of this fact at his accession. Not only did he never visit Hanover, he never left England during his reign.

George's long reign was initially controversial, plagued by financial problems and bad advice. His considerable influence on government was unpopular among Whigs, who accused him of having despotic ambitions, but his reputation was saved by two able ministers. Lord North, prime minister from 1770 to 1782, ably enacted George's policies but had to resign over American independence. Despite this setback, George's reign improved Britain's position on the wider imperial stage.

The controversial appointment of William Pitt the Younger at the age of only twenty-four in 1783 also proved beneficial for George, and he restored stability and fought successfully against France. Pitt fell out with the king, however, when he pushed for Catholic emancipation, and had to resign.

George was the first king to study science, was deeply interested in agriculture, and helped spread the Enlightenment to Britain. He built a Royal Collection of 65,000 books and founded the Royal Academy of Arts.

He was happily married to Charlotte, and had fifteen children, buying Buckingham Palace as a family home in 1761. But his recurring bouts of mental illness (now thought to be caused by porphyria) eventually meant his son, the Prince Regent, had to reign in his stead for his final ten years.

THE ENLIGHTENMENT
mid-18th–mid-19th centuries

"Superstition sets the whole world in flames; philosophy quenches them." (Voltaire, *Dictionnaire Philosophique,* 1764)

The Enlightenment was a far-reaching revolution in Western thought, underpinned by a belief in the power of reason. The geographic discoveries of the last two centuries; the Industrial Revolution; the growth of a merchant class; and scientific advances, particularly Newton's work—all contributed to influence society in Europe and America.

Writers such as Rousseau, Hume and Voltaire popularized Enlightenment ideals in essays and satires, Voltaire in particular having the ear of many European monarchs. The period also brought the beginnings of modern social and political ideas, as thinkers like Beccaria and Bentham advocated progressive causes, including prison reform and the ending of slavery. Adam Smith's work championed the free market while establishing economics as a science, and continues to influence modern policies. Theories and practices, particularly of power and the social order, were questioned—tradition was no longer an end in itself.

The Church was attacked as an enemy of reason—unsurprisingly, given its past treatment of scientists who challenged it. Enlightenment thinkers championed secular values, particularly the separation of Church and State.

The Enlightenment is one of the most important events in Western thought. It paved the way for the democracy, secularism and liberal capitalism of modern societies. Its principles defined two key events of the century—the French and American Revolutions.

THE INDUSTRIAL REVOLUTION, PART 1: FROM RURAL TO URBAN
*c.*1750–*c.*1830

The Industrial Revolution marked an enormous shift in Britain's economy and society. In eighty years, Britain went from being a mostly rural society to a modern urbanized industrial power.

It began with an agricultural revolution, peaking during the reign of George III. New farming technologies and greater understanding of plant nutrition increased agricultural production, which grew in tandem with the rising population. Rural unemployment led to a greater reliance on small-scale "cottage industries" producing consumer goods, which in turn gave way to larger factories.

The invention of the steam engine in 1769 revolutionized both farming and transport. Thousands of miles of railway track were laid in the early and mid-nineteenth century, allowing goods and people to be transported with ease and speed, while communications were made even faster by the advent of the telegram. New technologies, such as the power loom, transformed industry, and later, civil engineering, championed by Isambard Kingdom Brunel, flourished as ever-bigger bridges, tunnels and ships were constructed.

Although industrialization soon spread to Europe and America, it was Britain that led the way. The comparative stability of the government (almost all other European states went through some form of violent revolution during the "long nineteenth century") and its economic policy, influenced by the free-market ideas of Scots economist Adam Smith, created conditions that nurtured economic growth. The result was a major shift to modern capitalism. The British could now rely on home-grown manufactured goods, while the reach of the empire brought booming international trade.

THE BOSTON TEA PARTY
December 16, 1773

By the 1760s, British colonists in North America had become thoroughly disenchanted at being taxed by the Westminster Parliament, in which they had no representation, giving rise to the colonists' watchword of "No taxation without representation." They therefore boycotted heavily taxed imported tea, causing a financial crisis in the (British) East India Company. To save the company, the British government brought in the Tea Act, which allowed it to undercut the prices of colonial merchants and smugglers. This favorable treatment led to public protests in New York and Philadelphia—and to direct action in Boston.

By late 1773, angry colonists had prevented the East India Company merchantmen from unloading their cargoes in Boston harbor, despite the efforts of the port's pro-British governor. A standoff ensued, but on the night of December 16 a secret organization of American patriots known as the Sons of Liberty, disguised as Native Americans, boarded three of the tea ships and, with military precision, dumped their cargoes into the harbor. In all, some 51 tons of tea, valued at £10,000 (over $1.3 million today) ended up in the sea.

Two years later, Britain ended taxation of certain colonies, including the thirteen in North America, but the damage had already been done. The Boston Tea Party preceded numerous rebellious acts, ultimately proving to be one of the catalysts for the American Revolution, which in turn led to the establishment of the United States of America.

THE AMERICAN WAR OF INDEPENDENCE
1775–1783

Relations between Britain and its American colonies had deteriorated because of conflict over taxation, culminating in the Boston Tea Party. Major social changes in America had contributed further to this alienation. Initially, Britain refused to compromise over taxes and instead strengthened its military presence.

Armed hostilities began in 1775, when British forces attempting to suppress resistance in Massachusetts were attacked at Concord and Lexington. With no hope of a peaceful resolution, the Continental Congress (which included delegates from the thirteen British colonies in America) declared independence on July 4, 1776.

Though outnumbered and outgunned by the British and the Loyalists, the colonists had local knowledge, military experience and secret French support. A British invasion of New York that July was decisively repelled at Saratoga in 1777. The American Continental Army weakened the British presence in the south, but victory was only secured when the Continental Congress negotiated an open alliance with France in February 1778. Spain also lent its support, and a Franco-American force won the final major battle at Yorktown, Virginia, in 1781.

Now mired in international conflict, and without popular support for the American war, Britain was forced to withdraw. After two years of negotiations, the 1783 Treaty of Paris recognized the independence of the United States of America, and Britain made peace with France and Spain.

THE FRENCH REVOLUTIONARY WARS
1792–1802

In France, Enlightenment principles of freedom and equality contrasted with the repressive rule of Louis XVI. In 1789, armed citizens stormed the Bastille prison, and a revolution was sparked.

In Britain, the French Revolution was controversial. Its aims, if not its methods, echoed those of British parliamentary reformists, and many Whigs supported it. Criticism was led by Edmund Burke, a Whig who predicted that it would end in disaster. He was attacked by many liberals, especially Thomas Paine, who wrote *Rights of Man* in response. As the public support for reform increased, the government, fearing a similar revolution in Britain, began a crackdown. Paine was forced into exile, and reformists were harshly punished.

Louis XVI's execution in 1793—and the Reign of Terror in the year that followed, which saw some 17,000 French people executed, and another 25,000 or so dead—delegitimized the Revolution among mainstream reformists. European powers, including Britain, formed various coalitions against France, but were unable to stop aggressive French expansion, with Austria surrendering to France's brilliant young general, Napoleon Bonaparte, in 1797. Britain remained in the war, fending off Napoleon's attempted invasion of Egypt, but Napoleon's military reorganization led to further Austrian defeats. Britain briefly made peace with France in 1802, but the Napoleonic Wars followed almost immediately.

THE UNION WITH IRELAND ACT
July 2, 1800, effective from January 1, 1801

Ireland had been under English control since 1653 and the process of English conquest had been ongoing since 1169, but official union was long in coming and ultimately problematic.

The century following the Act of Union with Scotland (1707) saw religious tensions increase. After the Glorious Revolution, Irish Protestants, fearing a Catholic uprising, instituted the repressive Penal Laws, which denied Catholics full education and property rights. The Protestants controlled the Dublin Parliament, but they were also dissatisfied—Dublin was increasingly subordinate to London, which had imposed crippling restrictions on Irish trade.

Despite sectarian tensions, the French and American revolutions inspired pro-independence feeling on both sides, and many of the Penal Laws were relaxed. The United Irishmen included Protestants and Catholics, and campaigned for independence and religious tolerance. They rebelled in 1798, in the middle of a war with France, but were crushed despite late French assistance.

Prime Minister Pitt (the Younger) saw union as the only solution to this turmoil, and won Irish Catholic support by promising to repeal the Penal Laws. George III, however, felt compelled by his coronation oath to maintain them, leading Pitt to resign. The Parliaments were united in 1801—the Union forced through with bribes to many Irish MPs who became "Union Peers"—but the Penal Laws remained until 1829. Home Rule was still a hundred years away.

THE NAPOLEONIC WARS
1803–1815

I *never see a throne without feeling the urge to sit on it."*
(Napoleon Bonaparte, 1769–1821)

The peace of 1802 couldn't last long, and Britain renewed the war against France because of a dispute over the control of Malta. What was originally a counter-Revolutionary war had become an imperial conflict. Napoleon now controlled much of Europe, crowning himself emperor in 1804.

In 1805, Britain joined Austria, Russia and Sweden in the fight against France. Napoleon's preparations to invade Britain were put on hold while he campaigned against Austria and Russia, defeating them at Austerlitz. Britain's victory at Trafalgar allowed it to keep fighting alone, and also to control international trade.

Napoleon's attempt to control the Spanish throne provoked the Peninsular War in 1808 as Spanish rebels, joined by Portugal and Britain, resisted the French and eventually expelled them in 1814. The "Spanish ulcer" diverted forces from Northern Europe throughout the war. When Napoleon invaded Russia in 1812 his vast army was decimated by the bitter Russian winter. This defeat led to his fall and exile in 1814.

Napoleon returned and raised an army in 1815, sparking the final period of the war, the Hundred Days, which culminated in his defeat at Waterloo.

NELSON AND THE BATTLE OF TRAFALGAR
October 21, 1805

At the start of the Napoleonic Wars, Horatio Nelson (1758–1805) was already a leading commander and a national hero. He had joined the navy at twelve and risen through the ranks to win glorious victories at Cape St. Vincent, the Battle of the Nile and the Battle of Copenhagen. Appointed commander of the Mediterranean Fleet, Nelson was in charge of Britain's last line of defense when Napoleon threatened to invade and war broke out again in 1803.

The planned invasion involved a fleet under Vice Admiral Villeneuve, but Nelson barricaded Villeneuve in Toulon for two years. When Villeneuve escaped, Nelson chased him to Cádiz, where he was joined by Spanish ships but trapped by another British blockade. Villeneuve tried to escape on October 19, to land troops in Italy, but his fleet of thirty-three ships was intercepted two days later near the Cape of Trafalgar.

Nelson used a daring tactic to engage the enemy quickly. He sailed his twenty-seven ships in two groups toward the enemy line at right angles, exposing their own unprotected bows but destroying the French flagship and creating confusion.

He was shot (and eventually killed) by a sniper shortly afterward, but his plan was successful. The Franco-Spanish fleet turned back to Cádiz, but was hotly pursued. Twenty-two enemy ships, and not a single British one, were taken. There were 6,000 enemy casualties, and about 20,000 captured.

Trafalgar was Napoleon's final defeat at sea. It secured British naval dominance for the next century.

THE ABOLITION OF THE SLAVE TRADE
March 25, 1807

Between the sixteenth and nineteenth centuries, at least ten million African people were transported to the New World and sold as slaves. The British slave trade, pioneered by Drake and Hawkins, had produced a triangular system: slaves taken from Africa were traded for crops in America and the Caribbean, which were then traded for goods in Britain, which were shipped to Africa. The British economy flourished on the profits of slavery, with ports, factories and banks springing up in cities such as Bristol, Liverpool and London. Slave masters prospered, building town houses and stately homes.

But with the Enlightenment came a growing movement for the abolition of slavery. Not only was industrialization beginning to render it uneconomical, but slavery was also increasingly seen as deeply immoral, and more so as freed slaves found roles in society. Particularly influential was the Nigerian ex-slave Olaudah Equiano, who became a popular speaker and wrote about his experiences.

After twenty years of campaigning led by the MP William Wilberforce, a bill to stop the slave trade was introduced in 1805, but blocked by the House of Lords. The new Whig government of 1806 was determined to carry the measure, and the following year the Commons voted in favor of abolition, with only sixteen MPs voting against the ban.

It would take another thirty years for the trade to cease completely, and slavery itself wasn't abolished in the empire until 1838. Slavery in America was banned in 1862.

THE LUDDITES
1811–1812

The economic strain of the Napoleonic Wars affected people at all levels, especially the working class. Several poor harvests and soaring wheat prices combined with low wages to cause much unrest, with frequent riots caused by food shortages. Furthermore, the mechanization of the Industrial Revolution led to rising unemployment, particularly in the textile industry where new wide-framed looms could be operated by cheap, less highly skilled workers.

In 1811, activists known as Luddites broke into Yorkshire textile factories and destroyed the new wide-framed looms in order to save their jobs. They were named after Ned Ludd, a mysterious figure who destroyed two stocking frames in Leicestershire in 1779 and became a mythic hero to disenfranchised workers.

Luddite riots spread throughout the North and the Midlands in 1812. The government responded with the 1812 Frame Breaking Act, which made Luddite sabotage a capital crime. Uprisings were contained by the army, with a mass trial in York where many were executed or transported. Violent outbreaks continued, but petered out after five years.

The first Luddites were workers who rebelled against an economic system that ignored working-class concerns. Today, however, the term is synonymous with ignorant technophobia.

THE REGENCY
January 5, 1811–January 29, 1820

King George III's recurring bouts of mental illness, probably linked to porphyria, posed a problem to Parliament, which was divided as to who should rule the country—a parliamentary-appointed regent or the wayward George, Prince of Wales.

Prince George had several mistresses and had secretly married a Catholic widow, Maria Fitzherbert, in 1785. Under the Act of Settlement, this would have made him ineligible for the crown, but the marriage was invalid without his father's consent and was soon annulled. Marriage to his cousin, Caroline of Brunswick, was arranged in 1795, in return for the prince's huge debts being written off. The unhappy couple detested each other at sight and separated after the birth of their daughter, Princess Charlotte. They were never divorced, but George spent most of his time with mistresses or Maria Fitzherbert.

George III suffered a serious attack of madness in 1811, brought on by the death of his daughter, and never recovered. A Regency Bill was passed, appointing his son George Prince Regent.

The nine-year Regency was overshadowed by war, unemployment and civil unrest (including the murder of Spencer Perceval, the only British prime minister to be assassinated), but there were exciting developments in the arts under George's patronage. George's friend Beau Brummell introduced the "dandy" style to men's fashion, and John Nash designed Trafalgar Square, Regent's Park and Regent Street, as well as the exotic Royal Pavilion in Brighton.

WELLINGTON AND THE BATTLE OF WATERLOO

June 18, 1815

Arthur Wellesley, first Duke of Wellington (1769–1852), was an outstanding commander and statesman, who had previously won major victories in India and in the Peninsular War (1808–1814).

Napoleon had hit a losing streak, with disaster in Russia in 1812, a string of defeats in Europe, and defeat in the Peninsular War. He abdicated and was exiled to Elba in 1814. Wellesley was hailed as a hero, created Duke of Wellington and appointed ambassador to the restored French monarchy.

In 1815 Napoleon escaped from exile and marched on Paris, beginning the final period of the war (the "Hundred Days"). The allies prepared to invade and stop him, gathering their forces in Belgium in two armies: an Anglo-Dutch army under Wellington, and a larger Prussian force under Count von Blücher. Napoleon planned to exploit this division and began his attack on June 15, placing his army between the advance elements of the two allied forces. But he could not destroy Blücher's army, and on June 18, Wellington engaged the French at Waterloo, just south of Brussels.

Napoleon, anticipating an easy victory, attempted a diversionary flank attack that was unsuccessful—Wellington's forces, despite being slightly outnumbered, held firm. When Blücher's reinforcements arrived, the French were forced back. Napoleon mounted a final, desperate attack on the allied center, but Wellington formed his infantry into squares and defeated the offensive. A further French attack was repelled by the Prussians, and Napoleon was forced to retreat. Louis XVIII was restored, and Napoleon abdicated again and was banished to the island of St. Helena.

THE PETERLOO MASSACRE
August 16, 1819

Britain's victory against Napoleon came at a price. Shifting to a peacetime economy was difficult: Unemployment soared as munitions factories closed and troops returned, and high food prices were exacerbated by protectionist tariffs.

Discontent was growing, and not just for economic reasons. The crisis highlighted the lack of parliamentary representation for industrial cities, and a growing radical movement promoted reform. City dwellers gathered en masse to elect non-parliamentary representatives.

In 1819, one such meeting of 60,000 gathered at St. Peter's Fields, Manchester. Henry Hunt, a radical orator, was arrested by yeoman soldiers before he could address the crowd. When the demonstrators intervened, the inexperienced, possibly drunk, soldiers panicked and attacked them, prompting more soldiers to disperse the crowd by force. Several people were killed and hundreds wounded.

Widespread condemnation was exemplified in Shelley's poem *The Masque of Anarchy,* and the name "Peterloo" derisively contrasted the massacre with Wellington's victory. The government responded with the Six Acts, which restricted radical activity. This soon seemed justified by the Cato Street Conspiracy, a failed plot to kill government ministers.

The massacre is now considered a pivotal event in British political history, leading to reform in politics and policing.

GEORGE IV
1762–1830; crowned July 19, 1821

King George IV was known as the "First Gentleman of Europe," though for his manners rather than his conduct. Although his accession brought no real change in his power, the former Prince Regent toured his country in celebration. He was the first British monarch to visit Scotland and Ireland since the seventeenth century. George's marriage remained acrimonious—his estranged wife Princess Caroline was banned from his coronation and cut out of the Church of England's prayers for the royal family.

Believing, like his father, that the monarch should uphold the Protestant faith (and apparently ignoring his earlier marriage to a Catholic), he spent much of his reign opposing Catholic Emancipation. He was ultimately unsuccessful, and Parliament passed the Catholic Emancipation Act in 1829.

Despite George's influence on art and culture, he was deeply disliked by his subjects. His deplorable treatment of Princess Caroline only made her more popular, and there was a great outpouring of public grief when she died. He had become obese through his greed and self-indulgence and, as during the Regency, his reckless profligacy contrasted with the hardship caused by war and the Industrial Revolution.

George's daughter Charlotte had died in childbirth in 1817, so on the king's death the throne passed to his brother, who ruled as William IV. His short reign was dominated by reform issues, and his death in 1837 ended the Georgian period.

ROBERT PEEL AND THE METROPOLITAN POLICE
Metropolitan Police Act 1829

Britain after the Napoleonic Wars was suffering from social and political tensions aggravated by a heavy-handed government, which came to a head in the disastrous Peterloo massacre. Military force was not just oppressive, but also ineffective as law enforcement.

Sir Robert Peel (1788–1850), a moderate Tory, had already successfully established the Irish Constabulary in 1822. As Home Secretary in Lord Liverpool's government, Peel introduced the first regular police force in London, nicknamed "bobbies" or "peelers." Headquartered at Scotland Yard, the first thousand bobbies stepped out on September 29, 1829, in civilian uniform and armed only with truncheons. As crime rates rose nationwide, county forces were established on similar lines. In 1836, the force absorbed its predecessor the Bow Street Runners, and began using plainclothes detectives soon after.

Peel's tenure was distinguished by his social conscience. He engineered major prison reforms and reduced the use of capital punishment. Changes to the Corn Laws in 1828, and again in 1842, relaxed restrictions on imported grain, and the 1829 Catholic Relief Act allowed Catholics to vote and sit as MPs.

Peel was twice prime minister, in 1834–1835 and again in 1841–1846 when he passed major employment reforms and placed the nation's finances on a sound footing. He also reformed his party to establish the Conservative Party. However, he lost support when he repealed the Corn Laws in 1846, in an attempt to alleviate the Irish Potato Famine.

THE GREAT REFORM ACT
June 7, 1832

By the early 1800s, Parliament was corrupt, unrepresentative and in urgent need of reform. Monarchs and the aristocracy manipulated MPs, and seats were bought and sold. The qualification to vote varied across counties, but generally depended on wealth and land ownership. Political power remained in the hands of a landed elite, who mostly considered democracy equivalent to mob rule.

Furthermore, the distribution of parliamentary seats had not changed to reflect the urbanization of the Industrial Revolution— newly populous cities had no more influence than many villages. Most famous were the "rotten boroughs," which returned two MPs each despite tiny electorates. These constituencies, such as Gatton (with seven voters in 1831), could easily be politically dominated by local landowners and were themselves a form of property. Similarly, some monarchs had created tiny boroughs that would return favorable MPs.

But radicals like William Cobbett and Henry Hunt headed a growing reform movement, attacking the unfairness of the current system. Within Parliament, Whig reformers came to power for the first time in a generation and, despite strong Tory resistance, were able to convince a reluctant William IV that their Reform Bill should be passed. It increased the electorate from 450,000 to over 700,000 men, abolishing rotten boroughs and distributing seats more fairly. Subsequent Acts in 1867 and 1884 expanded suffrage to over half of British men. The property qualifications were removed completely in 1918, when women gained the vote.

VICTORIAN BRITAIN

QUEEN VICTORIA
1819–1901; crowned June 28, 1838

Princess Alexandrina Victoria of Kent was barely eighteen when she succeeded her uncle, William IV, on his death in 1837. Strong-willed by nature, the newly crowned Queen Victoria soon developed a sound understanding (though not without awkward moments) of constitutional matters, and although her reign saw the monarchy's influence diminish and power shift from the House of Lords to the Commons, it also witnessed the empire expand to make Britain the most powerful country in the world.

In February 1840, Victoria married her first cousin, Prince Albert of Saxe-Coburg and Gotha, by whom she had nine children. She never recovered from his early death from typhoid in 1861, and her grief-stricken seclusion (she famously wore black until her death) resulted in a brief loss of popularity. Under the guidance of close ministers, however, notably Disraeli, she gradually returned to public duties and again endeared herself to her subjects. Her popularity was reflected in the triumphant success of the Great Exhibition and in prodigious celebrations throughout the empire for her Golden and Diamond Jubilees.

Despite the numerous difficulties of her reign—among them the Crimean War, the Indian Mutiny, the Second Boer War, the intractable "Irish Question," and often severe poverty at home—Victoria remains Britain's most commemorated monarch for the countless advances her reign brought in science, commerce, invention, exploration, education, agriculture, policing, transport and the arts, and the establishment of many welfare programs, notably for poverty relief. She died, aged eighty-one, at Osborne House, Isle of Wight, the longest-serving British monarch to date.

DISRAELI AND GLADSTONE

Benjamin Disraeli, 1804–1881; Prime Minister February–
December 1868 and 1874–1880; William Ewart
Gladstone, 1809–1898; Prime Minister 1868–1874, 1880–
1885, February–July 1886 and 1892–1894

In general, the queen favored conservative prime ministers like
Lord Melbourne and Disraeli over more radical ones like Peel,
Palmerston and Gladstone. Disraeli was an especial favorite, charm-
ing her by laying on the flattery "with a trowel," unlike Gladstone,
who had a habit of addressing her "like a public meeting." After an
early career as a successful novelist, Disraeli entered Parliament on
a conservative platform in 1837, having initially stood, unsuccessfully, as a Radical. Twice chancellor and twice prime minister, he ac-
quired for Britain a half share in the recently built Suez Canal in
1875, and in 1876 he had Queen Victoria proclaimed Empress of
India. Tax increases and reverses in the Zulu and Second Afghan
wars led to the fall of his government in 1880 and he retired, dying
a year later.

Gladstone's political career spanned sixty-one years; he served as
prime minister four times. Although initially a Conservative, later
his name became forever synonymous with Liberalism, and he introduced several important improvements in women's rights, education and parliamentary reform. He also worked tirelessly to solve
the "Irish Question," though with limited success: His introduction
of the Irish Home Rule Bill split the party in 1886 and he finally resigned in 1894 after its defeat in the Lords. He was eighty-three.

Of the ten premiers of Victoria's reign, seven were born aristo-
crats. Disraeli accepted an earldom, and Gladstone declined one,
but neither man had been born to a seat in the Lords. They became,
arguably, the two greatest prime ministers of the Victorian era,
though they loathed each other all their lives.

THE INDUSTRIAL REVOLUTION, PART 2: THE COST TO SOCIETY
*c.*1770–*c.* 1850

With industrialization and the resultant growth in trade and capitalism, the population increased enormously, and the quality of life generally improved. Or at least this was the case for those who benefited directly from the boom.

Machinery and improved farming techniques resulted in a massive rise in rural unemployment as the new technologies made many laborers redundant. They migrated en masse to work in factories in the cities, quickly creating a large urban working class. Meanwhile, the mercantile middle class continued to grow and prosper, as major land ownership was no longer necessary to production.

In the cities social upheaval created new problems. Poverty was widespread among the urban working class, many of whom lived in slums with poor sanitation. Work was often unsafe and badly paid, with frequent use of child labor. With no kind of safety net, the unemployed and their families were forced into workhouses, doing menial work in grim conditions in exchange for basic accommodations. Industrial operations also caused severe air pollution, particularly in London where thick "pea-soupers" lowered visibility and endangered public health. Philanthropists, religious figures and writers highlighted the plight of the working classes, and these social issues influenced politics all through the 1800s.

VICTORIAN ARTS AND LITERATURE
19th century

Although the novel was by no means a Victorian invention, it flourished during this era. Stories were often published in serial form in mass-produced periodicals, lapped up by the emerging middle classes with the leisure and means to read for pleasure. The working classes were catered to with cheap and lurid penny dreadfuls. Serialization lent itself to sensational writing—with plenty of cliff-hangers, a large cast of characters and, often, unlikely plots—giving rise to the sprawling novels that were a feature of the period.

The great changes wrought in society by industrialization led many Victorian authors to dwell on social issues in their works, in contrast to the brooding introspection of the preceding Romantic period. Writers such as Charles Dickens and Elizabeth Gaskell exposed the plight of the urban poor, while George Eliot and Thomas Hardy reflected the harsh realities of life in rural society, and William Makepeace Thackeray satirized the snobberies and ambitions of the upper and middle classes.

The influence of Romanticism, however, lived on in the Gothic novels of Sheridan Le Fanu and Bram Stoker, and in the atmospheric sense of place of the Brontë sisters; and in the art world, in the haunting landscapes of J.M.W. Turner and John Constable. Later, Edward Elgar produced music "wonderful in its heroic melancholy," as Yeats put it.

Finally, in an age in which children were often sentimentalized (though child labor was still a reality of life for many), Beatrix Potter, Lewis Carroll, Anna Sewell and Robert Louis Stevenson, among others, wrote classics for the young that endure to this day.

INCOME TAX
1799, 1803 and annually since 1842

The financially draining war against Napoleonic France had left Britain nearing bankruptcy. With insufficient money to pay for military rations, the navy had threatened mutiny in 1797. Much of the country suffered poverty, with conflict growing between the manufacturing and agricultural classes. Against this backdrop, Prime Minister William Pitt "the Younger" introduced an income tax scheme in 1798 as a temporary measure to help beat France. Imposed the following year, it was inevitably unpopular.

The tax was applied in Britain, but not Ireland, at a rate of about ten percent on incomes over $16,500 per annum, and at a lower rate for smaller incomes. In the first year it raised $8.8 million, $5.8 million short of the government's target, but its introduction had set a precedent.

When Pitt resigned in 1802, the new prime minister, Henry Addington, repealed income tax during a brief peace with France, but on the resumption of hostilities in 1803 it was reintroduced. After Napoleon's defeat in 1815 the Chancellor of the Exchequer, Nicholas Vansittart, was forced by Parliament to revoke the tax "with a thundering peal of applause."

In 1842 Prime Minister Sir Robert Peel, although against the tax, reapplied it for three years at a rate of roughly three dollars for every hundred earned. In 1874 both Gladstone and Disraeli promised to repeal it, but it has stayed in place to this day. It remains, however, a temporary tax, reapplied by Parliament every April under the Finance Act.

THE IRISH POTATO FAMINE
1845–1851

In the summer of 1845 an air- and waterborne blight that had originated in North America rapidly destroyed much of Europe's potato crop. The effects were severe, but in Ireland, where a third of the population depended entirely upon the potato, they were catastrophic. The blight combined with wet weather to turn the crop to a putrid slime. The harvests of 1846 and 1847 were similarly devastated, leaving people starving and prone to typhus, cholera and dysentery. With no crop to sell they could not pay their rents to often absentee landlords, resulting in many evictions (though some landlords made real efforts to help their starving tenants). Only by 1850 was the worst of the famine over.

Since the Act of Union in 1801, Ireland had been governed from Westminster. In 1846 the Corn Laws—a protectionist measure placing prohibitive duties on imported grain—were repealed, but Ireland could not afford foreign grain. Government relief, mainly deliveries of substandard grain, was slow and ineffective. Private charities were forced to raise funds from overseas, though the money was often squandered.

Some 2.6 million Irish entered workhouses, and an estimated 1.5 million died from disease and starvation. The famine sparked mass emigration: The population of Ireland today, North and South combined, has still not reached its pre-famine level.

The "Great Famine" (or "Great Hunger") left a legacy of bitterness and mistrust toward Britain, not least because many wealthier, often Anglo-Irish, estates continued to export grain, meat and livestock to England at the height of the disaster.

VICTORIAN EXPLORERS AND INVENTORS
19th century

The British Empire reached its peak during the Victorian era, with around ten million square miles of territory added between 1815 and 1914. Explorers mapped uncharted land in the Canadian Arctic, Australia and, most famously, Equatorial Africa, with Sir Richard Francis Burton and John Hanning Speke making two major African expeditions in 1855 and 1857, becoming the first Europeans to reach Lake Tanganyika in 1858. Speke later discovered another great lake, which he named Victoria, believing it to be the source of the Nile. Scottish missionary David Livingstone also made numerous important discoveries in the African interior in his search for the Nile's source, and was the first European to see Victoria Falls (though he is perhaps best remembered for the line, "Dr. Livingstone, I presume?" supposedly uttered to him by a journalist, Henry Morton Stanley, sent to find Livingstone on his final expedition when he was missing, presumed dead).

The restlessness and energy of the Victorian era found other outlets in science, technology and engineering, with the civil and mechanical engineers George Stephenson and his son Robert building steam locomotives, public railways and bridges, and Isambard Kingdom Brunel designing several important bridges, tunnels, ships (including the first transatlantic steamship) and the Great Western Railway. Meanwhile, Michael Faraday made great developments in the understanding of electromagnetism and William Cooke and Charles Wheatstone patented the first commercial electric telegraph system in 1837, transforming personal communication. Other notable Victorian inventions include the postage stamp, a prototype of the modern vacuum cleaner and the negative/positive photographic process.

THE GREAT EXHIBITION
May 1–October 15, 1851

Billed as "the Great Exhibition of the Works of Industry of all Nations," and organized by, among others, Prince Albert, this was really a festival of British imperial dominance and prosperity as the optimism of the age spread throughout the country.

The Exhibition was the first true international fair, displaying nearly 14,000 of the world's finest artifacts, half of them British. It was held in Hyde Park in a showpiece building designed by the leading gardener and architect Joseph Paxton, a prefabricated glass-and-steel structure, covering nineteen acres, which *Punch* dubbed "the Crystal Palace."

Despite forecasts of failure, it was a resounding success. In the six months of opening some six million paying visitors came, many making their first train journey to do so. Queen Victoria made several visits, mingling with the crowds and nurturing public affection. The exhibition more than paid for itself, with large profits invested in the founding of the Victoria and Albert Museum and the Science and Natural History museums in Kensington. It influenced art and design, and helped to make "Victorian" a byword for national confidence.

After the Exhibition the Crystal Palace was moved piece by piece and reassembled on land at Sydenham Hill, south London, where it burnt down in 1936. Today, little remains except a few place names, the name of a football team and the name of the railway station built to bring visitors to the concerts, festivals and other entertainments held in the palace and its park.

THE CRIMEAN WAR
March 28, 1854–March 30, 1856

The war fought mainly in the Crimean Peninsula (modern Ukraine) against Imperial Russia brought the Irish war correspondent William Howard Russell to prominence. His exposés in *The Times* forced the government to improve conditions for servicemen, and to stamp out the use of corrupt civilian suppliers. The war also saw women accepted as nurses, notably Florence Nightingale and Mary Seacole.

In July 1853, following a diplomatic row with the Ottoman Empire over the Holy Land, Russia invaded Ottoman-controlled territory in the Crimea. Britain and her recent adversary, France, were opposed to Russian expansion, and when peace negotiations proved fruitless, war was declared.

Poorly equipped and supplied, thousands of allied troops succumbed to disease. Following public outrage, the British government permitted Nightingale to take female nurses to the Crimean front, where her attempts to alleviate suffering met with hostility from senior commanders. Scandalized, she used the press to expose the army's ill treatment, and established a hospital at Scutari; she then organized the barracks hospital after the allied victory at Inkerman (November 1854), dramatically reducing fatalities.

Partly because of such heroic disasters as the Charge of the Light Brigade at Balaclava (October 1854), the British Army eventually abolished the unfair practice of selling officers' commissions. The Battle of Balaclava also saw the successful charge of the Heavy Brigade, and the "Thin Red Line" (in Russell's phrase), in which the 93rd Highlanders defeated a Russian cavalry charge. The capture of Sebastopol in 1855 eventually led to a peace treaty in 1856.

THE INDIAN MUTINY
May 1857–March 1858

The Indian Mutiny began in the Bengal Army of the Honourable East India Company (HEIC), which then governed India. It developed into a widespread revolt against British rule, which threatened traditional Indian ways.

Trouble began when sepoys (Indian soldiers under British command) at Meerut refused to use cartridges greased with animal fat, offensive to their religions. Eighty-five members of the 3rd Bengal Light Cavalry were imprisoned. They were released by Indian supporters, and mutinies spread to units of the Bengal Army throughout central and northern India. The Madras and Bombay armies and the Gurkha regiments remained loyal, however, assisting British troops in suppressing the rebellions.

Delhi quickly fell to the rebels, becoming the focal point of the mutiny. With wholesale bloodshed on both sides, it took British forces three months to suppress 30,000 Delhi mutineers and four months to end the siege of the British residency at Lucknow. Cawnpore (now Kanpur) saw over two hundred British women and children massacred, but reprisals were often equally savage.

The Mutiny undoubtedly soured relations between Britain and India, later providing motivation for many Indian nationalists. After it, India came under the direct rule of the British Crown and the HEIC was nationalized (it was dissolved in 1874). To prevent further insurrections, Indian soldiers were demoted and issued with inferior firearms. Even so, Indian forces played a vital part in many subsequent British campaigns, including both world wars, until independence in 1947.

CHARLES DARWIN
1809–1882

Publication in 1859 of *On the Origin of Species by Means of Natural Selection*, by the English naturalist Charles Darwin, caused a sensation—the first edition sold out in a day. Most people still believed the biblical account of the Creation, and Darwin's theories on natural selection were widely attacked, although they also had eminent defenders. The principle of "survival of the fittest," however, reinforced Victorian optimism and belief in Britain's world superiority.

Darwin had studied medicine at Edinburgh University, but later changed to read divinity at Cambridge. He pursued a strong interest in natural history, and did not in the end take holy orders, as his father had hoped. In 1831 he joined a five-year scientific expedition, funded by the Admiralty, to the South Seas, South America and Australia on board HMS *Beagle,* a ten-gun brig-sloop of the Royal Navy. Despite a tendency to seasickness, he studied and recorded the wildlife, plants, fossils and geology of the many places visited and, on his return in 1836, put forward his theory of evolution, based on his observations. Despite often intense opposition, it rapidly gained widespread acceptance.

Darwin's subsequent works largely supplemented his principal theories; *The Descent of Man* (1871), in which he argued that man had evolved from the higher primates, is the best known. *On the Origin of Species* remains a leading study in natural philosophy, and one of the most influential scientific works of all time.

JOSEPH LISTER
1827–1912

Lister is known as "the father of modern antisepsis" for his incalculable contribution to the prevention of postoperative deaths. Initially studying the arts, he was soon drawn toward the scientific world of which his father, a pioneer of the compound microscope, was also a part. In 1852, he graduated with honors in medicine from the University of London, joining the Royal College of Surgeons.

After positions at Edinburgh and Glasgow universities, he was appointed surgeon at Glasgow Royal Infirmary. In 1861, he began to investigate the high death toll among postoperative patients.

While infection was, at that time, accounted for only by vague theories about "bad air" and "miasma," Lister sought a more detailed explanation. Deploying the grain of truth embedded in contemporary theory, and aware of Louis Pasteur's (generally ill-heeded) germ theory of disease, Lister's research helped to revolutionize medical practice.

Noting the use of carbolic acid (phenol) in deodorizing sewage, Lister tested Pasteur's theory by applying the chemical to surgical equipment before surgery, and to healing wounds after it. The outcome saw a substantial decrease in postoperation mortality.

Although initially regarded with suspicion, Lister's findings eventually received the attention they deserved. With the added impact of Florence Nightingale's revolution of nursing through the opening of her training school at St. Thomas's Hospital (July 1860), hospitalization ceased to be a virtual death sentence and became, as intended, a cure.

THE IRISH LAND ACT
1870

The Liberal William Gladstone won the general election of 1868 partly on a promise to resolve the "Irish Question." He was not widely supported, however, and a campaign of violence by the Fenians—a secret society of nationalist extremists—exacerbated the problem.

Although the state of Irish agriculture had improved since the Great Famine, the situation for Ireland's large but impoverished rural population, plagued by sectarian inequalities and several bad harvests, was still unstable. Gladstone defused Catholic resentment over paying tithes to the Anglican Church of Ireland by disestablishing it in 1869. He next acted to secure a better deal for Ireland's tenant farmers.

Gladstone's Irish Land Act of 1870 aimed to reform land ownership and weaken the dominance of landlords by restricting evictions, providing for compensation for improvements from landlords, and offering government assistance for tenants to buy land.

Government intervention failed to guarantee fair rents, however, and evictions and rent increases continued, with landlords undeterred by the threat of fines. These problems worsened with the end of a period of agricultural prosperity in the late 1870s, as tenant farmers could not compete with imports of cheap grain. Smallholders, encouraged by the Fenians, often sought violent revenge on their former landlords. The Fenians also supported Charles Stewart Parnell, leader of the eighty-five Irish MPs at Westminster, in organizing rent strikes and harvest boycotts, leading the government to introduce a Coercion Act to curb the violence in Ireland. Nevertheless, for the first time, Irish tenant farmers were guaranteed protection of their rights under law.

BRITAIN'S COLONIAL WARS
1837–1901

The late nineteenth century saw Britain engaged in almost constant conflict overseas. The list below is not exhaustive, but gives an idea of the extent of Britain's imperial commitments.

In 1837, British forces were engaged in putting down the Upper and Lower Canada rebellions. The majority of conflicts, however, occurred farther east: the First and Second Afghan wars (1839–1842 and 1878–1881); two Opium Wars fought over a trade dispute between the Honourable East India Company (HEIC) and the Qing Dynasty of China (1839–1842 and 1856–1860); the Anglo-Sind War in what is now Pakistan (1843); the First and Second Sikh wars in India (1845–1846 and 1848–1849); and the first of several Maori Wars (1845–1872) in New Zealand, as well as other campaigns like the Anglo-Persian War (1856–1857) and the Second Burma War (1852). Thereafter conflict tended more toward Africa: a punitive expedition to Abyssinia (now Ethiopia, 1868) between campaigns against the Xhosa in South Africa (1846–1879); the Zulu War (1879); the Basuto War (1880–1881) in what is now Lesotho, and the First Boer War; the Nile Expeditions (1884–1885 and 1897–1899); the Second Boer War; and the 1900 Ashanti Expedition in what is now Ghana.

Despite overwhelming superiority in equipment, firepower and training, on several occasions British troops suffered serious reverses at the hands of local forces they had been sent to subdue. Among the worst were at Gandamack (1842) and Maiwand (1880) in Afghanistan, and at Isandhlwana during the Zulu War (1879), as well as in both Boer wars.

EDUCATION FOR ALL
February 17, 1870

One third of British people were illiterate when Victoria became queen. Universal education had been of little concern to governments, and literacy and numeracy were seen as irrelevant to many working people. Only the sons of well-off families attended private schools. Since the 1780s, some working-class children had received free education from the Church and various charitable and philanthropic organizations, but its provision was patchy, especially in densely populated industrial areas. The Factory Acts of 1833 and 1844 had compelled employers of child workers to give daily schooling, but a basic education was far from being universal.

To maintain Britain's status as a world leader in the face of competition from countries like France and Prussia, with their established education programs, a new system was needed. There was also a political imperative: Since the Great Reform Acts of 1832 and 1867 had enfranchised more voters, literate people were able to learn, through the growing number of newspapers, about national issues before elections.

In 1870, therefore, the Liberal MP William Forster introduced the Elementary Education Act, which made compulsory a subsidized (in most cases) education for all children over five and under thirteen years old. Compulsion did not take effect until 1880 (a separate Act for Scotland in 1872 made it compulsory from the start).

Despite fears that universal education would foster unrest among the working classes, "Forster's Education Act" was a success, laying the foundations of a state-funded education available to all.

GORDON AT KHARTOUM
March 12, 1884–January 26, 1885

A hero of his age, the eccentric "Chinese" Gordon (1833–1885) was an officer of the Royal Engineers who fought in the Crimean War and the Second Opium War in China, earning his nickname while successfully defending Shanghai during the Taiping Rebellion in 1862. After postings in Sudan, China and South Africa, he was sent to Khartoum, Sudan, in 1884 to oversee the withdrawal to Egypt of Anglo-Egyptian forces, which were being threatened by Sudanese rebels led by the Mahdi, Muhammad Ahmad, a fanatical Muslim. Gordon refused to evacuate because of a shortage of boats to travel safely down the Nile, deciding instead to defend Khartoum rather than abandon Sudan to the Mahdists. He appealed to London for reinforcements, but the government delayed, despite public clamor for Gordon to be saved.

Under his skillful command Khartoum held out for ten months, but in January 1885, the city fell. British forces arrived two days too late: Gordon had been hacked to pieces and his head displayed in a tree.

At the news of the death of this warrior-martyr, public opinion turned against Gladstone and his government. Queen Victoria was so upset that she expressed her outrage in an unencrypted telegram to the prime minister: "The news from Khartoum are frightful, and to think that this all might have been prevented and many precious lives saved by earlier action is too frightful"—a rare example of a constitutional monarch publicly rebuking the government.

THE FIRST BOER WAR
December 20, 1880–March 23, 1881

The Boers (Afrikaners) were the fiercely independent descendants of the first Dutch settlers in South Africa. When, from the 1860s, rich deposits of gold and diamonds were discovered in their homelands, Imperial Britain's interests were roused, culminating in the annexation of the Transvaal, among other territories, in 1877. Paul Kruger, the uncompromising president of the Transvaal Republic, sought to maintain independence and the Boer way of life, which included resisting antislavery legislation. The goldfields attracted British prospectors, leading to constant Anglo-Boer friction, not least over the way the Boers treated black Africans. Britain claimed the area as a Crown Colony, whereupon an outraged Kruger issued a unilateral declaration of independence.

The Boer republics (the Transvaal and the Orange Free State) had no standing armies; instead, they relied on a kind of militia system, in which districts provided "commandos" to serve in times of conflict. Each member of a commando had to provide clothing, rations, a weapon and ammunition, and a horse. Tough and self-reliant, the Boers were expert hunters and trackers, fine horsemen and excellent marksmen, skilled in camouflage and concealment. The consequences, for the British troops, were salutary.

In a campaign lasting little more than ten weeks, British forces suffered several reverses, culminating in the crushing defeat at Majuba Hill on February 27, 1881, in which the commanding general, Sir George Colley, was killed. Gladstone's Liberal government, anxious to be conciliatory, acceded to self-government of the Transvaal under the British Crown, including nominal British control of African affairs.

THE SECOND BOER WAR
October 11, 1899–May 31,1902

In 1886, abundant deposits of gold and diamonds were discovered in the Witwatersrand hills of the Transvaal. Kruger maintained rigid independence, refusing civil rights to the vast number of foreign prospectors (many of them British) and overcharging them for supplies and transport. These *uitlanders* (foreigners) appealed to Queen Victoria herself for British protection. Under this pretext, Britain sought to annex the Transvaal and the other Boer heartland, the Orange Free State, and in 1899 war was declared.

The war went badly for the British at first. The Boers—having now established professional artillery corps—besieged several garrisons and there were severe defeats at Magersfontein, Stormberg and Colenso, while January 1900 saw another costly British reverse at Spion Kop. Lord Kitchener succeeded Lord Roberts as commander in chief of the imperial forces, and gradually the sieges were lifted and defeats inflicted upon the Boers in their turn. However, the fast-moving commandos maintained a guerrilla war, supplied by Boer civilians. Kitchener's scorched-earth policy in response saw Boer farms destroyed, food supplies cut off, and the introduction of "concentration camps" for sympathetic Boer civilians, where thousands died.

As the war turned in Britain's favor, Lord Salisbury's Conservative government emphasized the invincible empire, winning the "Khaki Election" of 1900 with an increased majority. The Treaty of Vereeniging in May 1902 promised the Boers eventual self-government, resulting in the Union of South Africa; Britain also offered $4.4 million toward postwar reconstruction.

THE ISSUE OF HOME RULE FOR IRELAND

April 8, 1886 and February 1893

Gladstone's crusade for a solution to the "Irish Question" continued with the Home Rule Bill debate in the Commons in 1886. His proposal was to allow domestic issues to be decided by a parliament in Dublin, with defense, foreign policy and international trade issues decided at Westminster, where Irish MPs would no longer sit. Ulster Protestants were opposed to a Catholic government in Dublin, however, and nationalists insisted that if Irish policy was to be decided in London, there should be representation. After sixteen days of debate the bill was lost by thirty votes, with the Liberals themselves split.

Seven years later Gladstone put forward a second Home Rule Bill; this passed the Commons, but was defeated in the House of Lords, since many feared an erosion of imperial power. Queen Victoria simply considered it disloyal to the Crown.

By 1910, Herbert Asquith's Liberal government was shored up by the Irish National Party, whose support had been bought with the promise of Home Rule. During two election campaigns in 1910 the "Irish Question" was buried, since mainland politicians and voters alike were more interested in social reforms and welfare.

The Home Rule Act was finally passed in 1914, under Asquith's Liberal government, though the implementation of the Act was postponed upon the outbreak of the First World War. It was not until 1921 that the "Irish Free State" achieved independence.

EDWARDIAN
BRITAIN

EDWARD VII
1841–1910; crowned August 9, 1902

Queen Victoria's eldest son, Albert Edward, the Prince of Wales, was nearly sixty when he succeeded her. Until then he had not been allowed much in the way of royal responsibilities, nor had he enjoyed access to state papers until he was in his fifties. His mother had despaired of his playboy tendencies, never forgiving him for a scandal with an actress that she believed hastened his father's death, but she may have misjudged Edward's character. In fact, on his accession he revitalized the monarchy after the somewhat dreary years of Victoria's long widowhood.

Edward's lifestyle was in marked contrast to that of Victoria. His large and genial figure reflected his appetites for rich banquets, port, cigars, horse racing, yachting and all manner of hedonistic pleasures. Although devoted to his elegant Danish wife, Queen Alexandra, he took many mistresses, notably Mrs. Alice Keppel and the actress Lily Langtry. He charmed people from all backgrounds, including union leaders and new Labour MPs—and even republicans.

Known as the "Uncle of Europe" and "Edward the Peacemaker," Edward was related to most European royalty, and his diplomatic skills and fluency in French and German did much to foster good foreign relations. He was the first British monarch to visit Russia and his state visit to France in 1903 culminated in the diplomatic understanding known as the "Entente Cordiale," putting an end to long-standing Anglo-French hostilities and forming the basis of the alliance that was to serve Britain in the First World War.

THE RISE OF LABOUR
1893–1908

By the end of the nineteenth century, a political revolution was quietly taking place in industrial areas of Britain. Led by Scottish miner James Keir Hardie, the newly created Independent Labour Party was successfully promoting the radical notion that working people could stand as parliamentary candidates.

The first working-class MPs were affiliated to the Liberals, and were known as "Lib-Labs." Thomas Burt and Alexander McDonald, both miners' leaders, were elected in 1874. In 1880, Henry Broadhurst, secretary of the TUC, joined them. By 1885 there were twelve Lib-Lab MPs who spoke on such issues as the introduction of eight-hour days for miners and whether police and troops should control industrial disputes.

Liberals had observed the electoral progress being made by their new colleagues, and realized they needed to take action to avoid splitting the working-class vote and giving ground to the Conservatives. In 1903, a secret Lib-Lab pact was made between the Liberal Herbert Gladstone and Ramsay MacDonald, Secretary of the Labour Representation Committee. It was agreed that Labour and Liberal candidates would not stand against each other in around fifty constituencies.

However, the Liberals failed to predict how the pact would affect their long-term electoral chances. Twenty-nine Labour candidates won seats in the 1906 general election, twenty-four of them unopposed by the Liberals. Working-class MPs were increasingly disengaging from the Liberal Party and a distinct Labour Party was emerging. When in 1908 the Miners' Federation voted to affiliate itself with Labour, the Lib-Lab pact—for the time being at least—became redundant.

THE SUFFRAGETTES
1903–1914

Despite small but significant gains in women's rights to education, property ownership and legal representation in the latter half of the nineteenth century, women were still specifically excluded from the electorate. Well-connected ladies began, unsuccessfully, to lobby MPs, setting up small "suffragist" societies throughout the country that eventually joined to become the National Union of Women's Suffrage Societies (NUWSS) in 1897, under the leadership of Millicent Fawcett.

Frustrated by the slow progress of NUWSS, the radical activist Emmeline Pankhurst established the militant Women's Social and Political Union (WSPU) in 1903 to carry out high-profile and violent acts of protest. These so-called "suffragettes" burnt churches and letter boxes, ransacked men-only golf courses and cricket pavilions, slashed works of art, set off bombs and chained themselves to the railings of Number 10. In 1913, the movement claimed its first martyr: Emily Davison, who jumped to her death under the king's horse on Derby Day in an attempt to pin suffragette colors on it.

Despite the ensuing headlines, MPs stood firm. Force feeding was introduced to hunger-striking suffragettes in prisons, and the "Cat and Mouse Act" was passed in 1913 to allow hunger strikers to be released on license, thus preventing them dying in captivity and gaining public sympathy.

It took the First World War to change public opinion, and it was not until 1918 that women won a limited right to vote and 1928 when they could vote on equal terms with men.

THE SINKING OF THE *TITANIC*
April 14–15, 1912

T*he sounds of people drowning are something that I cannot describe to you, and neither can anyone else. It's the most dreadful sound and there is a terrible silence that follows it."* (Eva Hart, *Titanic* survivor)

The "unsinkable" RMS (Royal Mail Steamer) *Titanic* was the largest passenger liner in the world, owned by the White Star Line and built in Belfast. The 77,000-ton steel ship was the last word in luxury, with its own swimming pool, gymnasium, Turkish bath, libraries and squash court.

On the fourth night of her maiden voyage from Southampton to New York, the *Titanic* hit an iceberg south of the Grand Banks of Newfoundland, and sank in two hours and forty minutes. Only 706 people survived, of whom the majority were first-class passengers. Many lifeboats were lowered only half filled with people; there were, in any case, not enough lifeboat places to go around. Only two of the eighteen launched lifeboats turned back to rescue their fellow passengers, many survivors fearing they would be pulled down by the suction from the sinking ship, or by people trying to climb into the boats. In total, 1,517 people died, in what is still one of history's worst peacetime maritime disasters.

The tragedy of the *Titanic* was a blow to Britain's confidence, previously high on the imperial superiority and engineering achievements of the Victorian era, and became forevermore a poignant symbol of the fallibility of modern technology.

THE FIRST WORLD WAR YEARS

THE FIRST WORLD WAR
August 4, 1914–November 11, 1918

The early years of the twentieth century saw some major shifts in alliances in Europe. Germany was emerging as a superior industrial and military power, and came to replace France as Britain's main threat. The two principal alliances were the Entente Powers (Britain, France and Russia), joined by Italy in 1915 and the United States in 1917; and the Central Powers (Germany, Austria-Hungary and the Ottoman Empire). An arms race developed in response to German naval expansion and in 1906 Britain launched the revolutionary *Dreadnought* battleship.

War was triggered on June 28, 1914, when a Bosnian Serb student assassinated Archduke Franz Ferdinand, heir to the Austrian throne, in Sarajevo. Austria-Hungary retaliated against Serbia and, like a falling set of dominoes, one by one the other European countries became involved in the crisis, as the complex web of alliances came into force. Germany declared war on France on August 3, and invaded neutral Belgium the same day. Britain was left with little option but to come to its Allies' defense.

Trench warfare in France was protracted and devastating, with troops subject to a terrifying ordeal of gunfire, poison gas, shell shock, mutilation, rats and disease. Over two million men responded to Lord Kitchener's call for volunteers. More troops were needed by 1916 and conscription was introduced.

At sea, the German U-boat threat was so successful in cutting off British food supplies that surrender was briefly considered in 1916. For the first time war was fought by air, and southern England suffered zeppelin bombing raids. Fighting even extended into Asia and Africa, and three million Commonwealth soldiers rallied to support Britain. In Turkey in 1915, thousands of Anzac and British soldiers perished at Gallipoli.

By 1917, the war was at a stalemate. In April that year, however, the United States joined the Allies, changing the balance of hostilities dramatically. Germany realized that it must win on the Western Front before American superiority in manpower and matériel could take effect. Peace with Revolutionary Russia in March 1918 meant that German troops could be transferred from the Eastern Front, so on March 21 General Erich Ludendorff launched a sudden, massive offensive against British and French armies on the Western Front. For a time the situation looked bleak for the Allies. However, with American troops now playing an important role, the Allied line held, and by mid-July the German effort was spent. Now the Allies counterattacked, piercing the "impregnable" Hindenburg Line in September, and sending the demoralized Germans into retreat. The deadlock of more than four years had ended. On November 7 Germany surrendered, and at eleven A.M. on November 11 the Armistice came into effect.

The "War to End All Wars" was fought on an unprecedented scale. Sixty million European soldiers were mobilized, and there were over 20 million casualties, both military and civilian. No British citizen was untouched by the war: Women worked in factories, food was rationed, children helped on farms and taxes were increased. The legacy of the tragic loss of life has been handed down through the generations and still resonates today.

THE SINKING OF THE *LUSITANIA*
May 7, 1915

RMS *Lusitania* was a luxury British ocean liner, affectionately known as the "Greyhound of the Seas." On May 1, 1915, she left port in New York bound for Liverpool with 1,959 people on board.

Sea travel was, of course, not without risk during the war, and the threat from U-boats in British waters was well known, but it was believed that the *Lusitania*'s speed would protect her from attack. As a precaution, Captain Turner posted extra lookouts and swung the lifeboats out as they entered the dangerous waters of the Irish Channel, but due to fog he also controversially ordered the ship to slow and steer straight ahead. She was a sitting duck.

As she drew close to Ireland, the German submarine *U-20* launched a torpedo into her hull. She sank in eighteen minutes, killing over 1,100 civilians, including almost 100 children.

America was outraged that 128 of her citizens lost their lives in a war in which they were not involved. Tensions heightened between America and Germany and public opinion began to sway in favor of America joining the war, which it would do within two years. Bowing to worldwide outrage, Germany withdrew its "sink on sight" policy in September that year, reintroducing it on February 1, 1917.

THE EASTER RISING
April 24–29, 1916

Over one hundred years after the Dublin Parliament had been abolished, the 1914 Home Rule Act finally reinstated a limited form of self-government in Ireland. However, many Protestants in the northeast of Ireland were fiercely opposed to southern Catholic-dominated rule, fearing they would be marginalized. An earlier amendment to the Act had proposed Ireland would be partitioned, with certain northern counties being temporarily excluded from Home Rule, but this was not enough to appease either side and soon Ireland was on the brink of civil war. British peacekeeping troops were mobilized, but many were Unionist sympathizers who refused to fight Ulstermen.

Disaster was averted as Irish affairs were overtaken by events in Europe. Implementation of the Act was postponed, and men on both sides joined the war effort against Germany. However, while Britain was preoccupied elsewhere, radical republican groups led by the Irish Republican Brotherhood (IRB) seized the opportunity to plan an uprising in Dublin. Despite 20,000 German-supplied rifles being intercepted by the Royal Navy, the rebellion proceeded, with an Irish provisional government proclaimed from Dublin's General Post Office. After six days of fierce fighting there were several hundred dead and parts of Dublin lay in ruins.

Fifteen republican leaders were swiftly tried and executed and some 1,800 rebels were interned. The rising itself failed, but succeeded in radicalizing public opinion; the "1916 martyrs" provided a potent legacy. Moderate opinion turned against the British, laying the foundations for the Irish War of Independence.

THE BATTLE OF THE SOMME
July 1, 1916–November 18, 1916

By the end of 1915 the war had reached stalemate. Commander in chief Sir Douglas Haig vowed to seize the initiative by mounting an Allied offensive on the twelve-mile front by the River Somme, partly in order to distract German attention from the French-defended city of Verdun.

A week of shelling preceded the attack to weaken the German lines, leading to the assumption that Allied forces would then be able to overwhelm the enemy on foot. But the Germans were heavily fortified and well prepared, and when the British troops advanced at walking pace, they were gunned down in their thousands. On the first day alone, 19,240 British soldiers died. Many were untrained volunteers, some still teenagers. Any gains were rapidly lost due to inadequate communications and lack of reinforcements.

Undeterred, Haig pressed on, ordering more and more men to go "over the top." Eventually Britain put tanks into action—their first appearance in battle—but they were of limited use in the muddy terrain. In total there were some 420,000 British casualties. Germany also suffered massive losses and was forced back, but was never in danger of defeat.

Conditions on the front were hellish, with bodies left to decompose, waterlogged trenches, lice, rats, disease, and the constant fear of death. Haig's long-awaited breakthrough never came. As winter weather set in, he abandoned the campaign.

The Battle of the Somme is the bloodiest on British record. After five months of slaughter, the Allies had advanced only five miles.

DAVID LLOYD GEORGE
1863–1945; Prime Minister 1916–1922

David Lloyd George was one of a new radical breed of Welsh Liberals, and was the youngest MP in the house when he entered Parliament in 1890. A natural social reformer, he developed a welfare system for society's most vulnerable, including school meals for the poor, old age pensions, help for the unemployed and national health insurance.

As chancellor he presented the "People's Budget" in 1909, funding the reforms by increasing income tax and death duties. Naturally, the Lords rejected this, leading to the Parliament Act of 1911 that finally reduced their power of veto.

While acting as Minister of Munitions from 1915, Lloyd George became increasingly critical of the Liberal Prime Minister Asquith, who was heading the wartime coalition government. He replaced Asquith in December 1916, and was an energetic leader, introducing conscription and playing a central part in later peace negotiations.

The "Welsh Wizard" won the patriotic vote in the election immediately after the war on his "land fit for heroes" ticket, promising further reforms. But he had helped to divide the Liberal party, which never completely recovered, and when the Conservatives withdrew from the coalition in 1922, he resigned.

THE 1918 FLU PANDEMIC

In 1918, war was not the only mortal enemy facing the country; a global flu pandemic was also causing widespread devastation. Unusually, it affected fit adults rather than the more vulnerable young and old. About a quarter of a million British people died from the disease.

In the spring of 1918, thousands of soldiers on the Western Front suffered sore throats, headaches and loss of appetite, their immune systems likely weakened by trench conditions. At first, sufferers recovered in three days. However, soon doctors identified a new virulent strain of the virus. Spain, France, the Middle East, India and China were variously accused of being the source, though recent research indicates it came to the trenches via a group of American soldiers from Kansas. By the summer, symptoms worsened and soldiers started to die from pneumonia or blood poisoning. By September, the German army was debilitated and the disease had spread, killing over 400,000 German civilians that year.

The first cases in Britain appeared in Glasgow in May 1918 and the epidemic spread quickly. In vain, authorities sprayed streets with chemicals, and antigerm masks became popular. No corner of the world was immune. Nearly 450,000 Americans had died by early December. India was worst hit, perhaps infected by the many Indian doctors who had served in the war; over sixteen million Indians died of the virus. The estimated worldwide death toll ranges from fifty to seventy million people, many times more than that of the First World War.

THE TREATY OF VERSAILLES
June 28, 1919

Following the 1918 Armistice, Prime Minister Lloyd George attended the Paris Peace Conference and signed the Versailles Treaty, which formally agreed to the end of hostilities. Leaders of thirty-two states attended, though Britain, America and France dominated. France wanted Germany brought to its knees so that it could never start another war, while Lloyd George was more cautious, fearing an embittered, destitute Germany might allow itself to become a gateway to Communism in Europe.

Germany signed the treaty under protest, accepting full responsibility for the war. In the subsequent redrawing of the map of Europe—in which the old nation of Poland was re-created—Germany lost colonies, access to much of its coastline and resources, and about four million citizens. Its armed forces were drastically limited, and it was made to pay $9.7 million reparations to civilian populations affected by the war, though no German war leaders were put on trial.

As part of the treaty, the League of Nations was formed, promoted by U.S. President Woodrow Wilson (though the United States itself did not end up joining). This was an international body whose aim was to promote democracy and avoid future war by means of diplomacy.

For Britain and France the treaty was generally seen as a diplomatic success. However, the German people were united in their resentment against it, and in a few short years both the aims of the League of Nations and the terms of the Treaty of Versailles lay in tatters.

THE
INTERWAR
YEARS

THE AMRITSAR MASSACRE, INDIA
April 13, 1919

The postwar world was in flux, with the new League of Nations setting many countries on the path to "self-determination" (independence). India won certain concessions to home rule, but the Government of India Act (1919) kept law, order and taxation firmly in British hands, provoking widespread public demonstrations. After all, 1.5 million Indians had fought in the trenches; was the continuing humiliation of dependency on the British to be their reward?

By spring 1919, matters had come to a head, with an escalation of violent incidents around the country. On April 13, a nationalist crowd of Punjabis gathered in Amritsar, defending their right to assemble at a holy shrine. The local commander, Brigadier-General Reginald Dyer, decided to "teach a moral lesson to the Punjab." Without warning, he ordered his troops to fire into the terrified crowd. Official reports state 379 unarmed men, women and children were killed, some trampled to death in the confusion, with a further 1,200 injured in the ten-minute attack. Other contemporary accounts claim there were many more victims. Asquith denounced it as one of the worst outrages in British history, but the British public largely believed a second Indian Mutiny had been averted. Dyer was later forced to resign his commission.

This massacre enraged an India that had already lost faith in British promises. It became a turning point for the struggle for independence: In 1920, Mahatma Gandhi began a new campaign of mass civil disobedience that finally helped to end British rule.

THE BRITISH COMMONWEALTH
The Statute of Westminster, December 11, 1931

Throughout the First World War, Britain had been strongly supported by its former colonies, including the self-governing "Dominions" of Australia, New Zealand, South Africa, Canada and Newfoundland. Their leaders had been members of the War Cabinet, and they were acknowledged as "sovereign nations" and independent members of the newly formed League of Nations.

The 1931 Statute of Westminster effectively granted independence to these countries (along with the Irish Free State) for the first time, giving them equal status and allowing them membership of the British Commonwealth of Nations. This was a voluntary association of former colonies headed—but not ruled—by the British monarch. Gradually other former colonies joined the Commonwealth on gaining independence. The old empire was slowly being dismantled; in its place was a "free association" dedicated to equality, democracy, liberty, peace and free trade.

India, Britain's largest colony, was an exception. It had not achieved self-government before the war and remained a Dominion under the India Act of 1935 until it achieved independence in 1947.

PALESTINE AND MESOPOTAMIA
April 25, 1920

O f the many momentous decisions made in the aftermath of the First World War, one was to have particularly far-reaching consequences: The partitioning of the Ottoman Empire, a super-power that once controlled much of southeastern Europe, the Middle East and North Africa. After its defeat in the war, the Ottoman government collapsed completely, and in 1920 the League of Nations granted France and Britain the right to govern its former territories, with Britain gaining mandates over Palestine and Mesopotamia.

Britain's solution for Mesopotamia was to appoint Faisal Hussein as king of the region (renamed Iraq) in reward for his father's wartime support. As for Palestine, Britain divided this area in two, creating the Emirate of Transjordan east of the Jordan River, to be ruled by Hussein's brother Abdullah, and the Palestine Mandate to the west.

It was a solution that pleased no one. The British had previously proposed international administration for Palestine; they had also promised to create an independent Arab state; what's more, they had similarly vowed to support the right for Jewish people to establish a "national home" there, in the Balfour Declaration of 1917. Britain assumed the 85,000 Jews and 600,000 Arab Palestinians could coexist peacefully: sadly, it set the stage for many decades of conflict in the Middle East.

THE PARTITION OF IRELAND
The Anglo-Irish Peace Treaty, December 6, 1921

Following Britain's heavy handling of the Easter Rising in 1916, Irish voters overwhelmingly supported the separatist political party Sinn Fein in elections two years later. The MPs refused to take their seats in Westminster and set up their own Parliament in Dublin, the Dáil Éireann. Under Michael Collins, Sinn Fein's military arm, the IRA, waged a savage guerrilla war of independence from January 1919 to July 1921. The British paramilitary forces, known as the Black and Tans after their uniform, were also renowned for their brutality, and their atrocities alienated moderates on both sides.

A political solution to the "Irish Question" had to be found. In December 1921, Lloyd George negotiated an Anglo-Irish Treaty that gave limited self-government to the six counties of Ulster to the north (though their MPs were still sent to Westminster). The remaining twenty-six counties to the south were given Dominion status and became the Irish Free State, ruled by the Dáil Éireann.

However, hard-line nationalists opposed the treaty, believing all of Ireland, including Ulster, should become a Republic. The result was a two-year civil war between rival IRA factions, bringing about yet more bloodshed and the death of Michael Collins.

Aspects of the treaty were gradually dismantled, until the south declared itself the Republic of Eire in 1937, refusing to acknowledge the fact of Partition. Britain did not formally acknowledge the Republic until 1948.

THE GENERAL STRIKE
May 3–12, 1926

Britain, once the world's foremost coal exporter, could not compete with cheap imported coal after Germany's return to the international coal market in 1925. Britain's coal seams were depleted after the war and productivity was falling. With the industry in disarray, mine owners proposed reducing their workers' wages. The Trades Union Congress (TUC) promised to support the miners, so Stanley Baldwin's Conservative government intervened and vowed to subsidize wages for nine months: a short-lived victory for the working class. Lord Samuel's subsequent Royal Commission into the industry rejected nationalization, proposing a withdrawal of the wage subsidy in return for better conditions and investment in new machinery, while the mine owners continued to press for longer working hours and lower pay.

The TUC announced a General Strike in support of the miners, and three million sympathetic workers downed tools in such key industries as transport, docks, printing, building, ironworks and steel. Essential services such as health care and food transport stayed working, so overall disruption was minimal. Without newspapers (except Chancellor Winston Churchill's personally edited *Specials*), the new BBC made its mark, providing news and effectively preventing panic.

After nine days, the TUC capitulated to Lord Samuel and agreed to end the strike. However, many miners continued to stay out for several months, until poverty forced them back. The returning miners had to accept lower wages and longer hours, and many could not find work again. In 1927, Baldwin introduced the Trade Disputes Act, banning general strikes in the future.

RAMSAY MACDONALD
1866–1937; Prime Minister January–November 1924, 1929–1935

The charismatic Scot Ramsay MacDonald was Britain's first Labour prime minister. With the help of his wife's small private income, he had risen above his humble, illegitimate origins to be elected as an MP for the newly formed Labour party in 1906, and became party leader in 1911.

Opposed to Britain entering the First World War, MacDonald resigned his chairmanship in 1914, becoming leader again in 1922, by which time Labour had replaced the Liberals as the main Tory opposition. In 1924 Labour won the election, but only with Liberal support. The excitement at achieving office for the first time quickly evaporated as Labour lost power within the year, plagued by press rumors and opposition propaganda about the Communist threat. But MacDonald had proved that Labour could govern effectively, and had shown his flair at handling international matters.

Returning to power in 1929, the MacDonald government succumbed to the pressure of the Great Depression and cut public expenditure, including unemployment benefits. With a split cabinet, MacDonald formed a coalition government in 1931, an act that most of his Labour colleagues considered a betrayal of the party he had helped create. MacDonald led the coalition, but the new national government was Conservative in all but name.

Weakened, and with declining health, MacDonald survived as PM until 1935. The Conservatives, along with his own party members, treated him with contempt, although he retained considerable influence in foreign affairs. He died two years later on a recuperative voyage to America.

WOMEN'S SUFFRAGE
1918–1928

The suffragette terror campaign of the early twentieth century wound down during the First World War when the WSPU softened its militant line and urged women to join the armed forces or work in industry. Many suffragettes, notably Sylvia Pankhurst, became peace campaigners. But the overall effect of war on women's role in society was enormous. Women from all backgrounds contributed to the effort, working on farms, in munitions factories and as nurses, which did much to promote their crusade for enfranchisement.

After the war, Prime Minister Lloyd George could no longer deny that the perception of women's capabilities had changed, and in 1918 an Act was passed enabling certain women over the age of thirty to vote.

With suffrage also came the right to stand for election, and at the 1918 General Election, 17 women—many of whom had been suffragettes—stood out of 1,623 candidates. Only one was successful, Constance Markievicz for Sinn Fein, though as an Irish nationalist she refused to take her seat in Westminster. In December 1919, Nancy Astor won her husband's seat for Plymouth Sutton when he moved up to the Lords, and became the first female MP to take the oath.

The Representation of the People Act 1918 was a great milestone on the path of women's rights. But it would take another ten years before all women over twenty-one could vote on equal terms with men.

FLEMING DISCOVERS PENICILLIN
September 28, 1928

The Scottish bacteriologist Alexander Fleming (1881–1955) served in the Army Medical Corps during the First World War, working in field hospitals where he observed many deaths from septicemia. Fleming proved that the antiseptics commonly prescribed to treat the infected wounds did more harm than good, though army doctors continued to use them. He returned from the war to St. Mary's Teaching Hospital in London, where he took up the post of Professor of Bacteriology.

Not the tidiest of technicians, Fleming often left the cultures he was developing lying about his laboratory. Returning one day after a long holiday, Fleming noticed that many of his discarded culture dishes contained a mold, encircled by a bacteria-free area. He identified the active substance as penicillin, and further research showed it could kill other bacteria, such as the ones that caused meningitis, diphtheria, scarlet fever and pneumonia.

Two other scientists, Australian Howard Florey and Ernst Chain, a refugee from Nazi Germany, developed Fleming's discovery so that it could be produced as a drug. They shared the Nobel Prize in Medicine in 1945. Initially, supplies of the "wonder drug" were limited, but by the 1940s penicillin was mass-produced in America, hailed as one of the greatest medical advances ever made.

EDWARD VIII AND THE ABDICATION
1894–1972; reigned January 20–December 10, 1936

K ing George V's son, Edward, the Prince of Wales, enjoyed immense popularity due to his service in the First World War and his sympathy for the poor, not to mention his noble good looks, playboy bachelor status and world tours. However, the public was not aware of his numerous affairs with married women, including one twice-divorced, socially ambitious American socialite who was to change the course of British royal history: Mrs. Wallis Simpson.

Acceding to the throne in January 1936, Edward declared his intention to marry Mrs. Simpson in a meeting with Prime Minister Stanley Baldwin in November of that year. But the Church of England disapproved of remarriage after divorce and, as Supreme Governor of the Church, the king was expected to live by its rules. Although rumors of the affair had been reported abroad and in London society, the British press did not break the story until December 3. In the face of a constitutional crisis, Baldwin told Edward that if he married against the government's wishes, he would be forced to call an election. On December 10, Edward duly abdicated.

He broadcast his decision to the world on the BBC the following evening, famously declaring that it would be impossible for him to continue as king "without the help and support of the woman I love."

Retitled the Duke of Windsor, Edward married Wallis Simpson in June 1937. They lived in exile, mainly in France, until their deaths. Edward VIII still remains the only British monarch to have voluntarily given up the crown.

GEORGE VI
1895–1952; crowned 1937

The Duke of York, or Prince Albert as he was then known, neither wanted nor expected to become king. Beset by shyness and an acute stammer, he was nevertheless thrust into the role as a result of his older brother's abdication. He was to be the third king of the House of Windsor and the third king of 1936.

Despite his initial fears, the new King George VI and his queen, the former Lady Elizabeth Bowes-Lyon, quickly gained the respect of both the government and public alike. They made successful state visits to France, Canada and the United States and, during the dark years of the Second World War, their visits to bomb sites and munitions factories helped boost morale at home. George himself had seen active service in both the navy and the Royal Air Force during the First World War, and at the height of the Blitz he founded the George Cross for civilian acts of "the most conspicuous courage in circumstances of extreme danger." He and Queen Elizabeth refused to leave London during the bombing, despite the threat to their safety.

His reign saw the disintegration of the British Empire, and he was the last Emperor of India and nominally the last king of Ireland. He was succeeded by his eldest daughter, the current Queen Elizabeth II.

SIR OSWALD MOSLEY AND THE FASCISTS

British Union of Fascists, October 1, 1932–May 30, 1940

After stints as a Conservative and Independent MP, the well-connected and ambitious Sir Oswald Mosley became a minister in MacDonald's Labour government. However, his colleagues rejected his plans to combat the industrial depression of the inter-war years, so Mosley created a breakaway socialist movement called the "New Party." After unsuccessfully contesting the 1931 general election, Mosley visited fascist Italy, where Mussolini's state control appeared to be the solution to unemployment. Impressed, he disbanded the New Party and established the British Union of Fascists (BUF).

The BUF was anticommunist and anti-Semitic, claiming a 50,000-strong membership at its peak. Mosley and his quasi-military followers, the Blackshirts, led marches through London's largely Jewish East End, provoking riots between the Fascists and the counterprotestors: a united front of local Jews, socialists, Irish and communists. The government reacted by passing the Public Order Act of 1936, banning political uniforms and private armies, which curtailed the BUF's activities.

Mosley admired the Nazis and in 1936 secretly married his second wife Diana Mitford in the presence of Hitler, at Joseph Goebbels' Berlin house. He campaigned for peace after the outbreak of war, until in 1940 he was interned in Holloway Prison, along with other active Fascists. Mosley was released in 1943 to much opposition, and he and his wife lived for the rest of their lives in France, near their close friends the Duke and Duchess of Windsor.

MUNICH AND THE LEAD-IN TO THE SECOND WORLD WAR
1938 and 1939

The rise of fascist dictatorships in Europe dominated British foreign policy in the 1930s. In Germany, the Nazi leader Hitler set about flouting the despised Versailles Treaty that had so humiliated the nation, and began a massive campaign of remilitarization. But with the horrors of the First World War still fresh in people's memories, both Britain and its ally France were reluctant to become involved in another war.

Despite the increasingly grave international situation, Prime Minister Neville Chamberlain made every effort to meet Hitler's "reasonable" demands in order to avoid handing him an excuse to declare hostilities. Likewise, the League of Nations did nothing to prevent Hitler's troops marching into Austria in 1938. Emboldened, Hitler moved to reclaim Sudetenland, a strategically important part of Czechoslovakia with a large German population. Chamberlain met Hitler three times over the Sudetenland crisis, culminating in the Munich Conference in September 1938, attended by Germany, France, Britain and Italy. To general public approval, Chamberlain returned home declaring "peace in our time," believing he had succeeded in averting war by conceding Sudetenland to Germany. In return, Hitler had promised not to make further territorial demands.

In March 1939, however, Hitler showed his contempt for the agreement and took the rest of Czechoslovakia. Britain abandoned its policy of appeasement and promised to defend Poland, the next target in Hitler's sights, should it be invaded. In August 1939 this came to pass, and on September 3, Britain declared war on Germany.

THE SECOND WORLD WAR

GERMANY INVADES
September 1, 1939–June 22, 1940

Still smarting from the terms of Versailles, Hitler began his expansionist drive on a wave of nationalist fervor. After his occupation of Sudetenland, he invaded Poland on September 1, 1939, ordering 1.5 million troops into the country. Towns and cities were attacked by the Luftwaffe, and German tanks, infantry and cavalry converged on the capital, Warsaw. That day, France and Britain issued a fruitless ultimatum to Germany to withdraw its troops, and on September 3 war was declared.

On September 17, Soviet forces began pouring into Poland, acting under the secret terms of the Nazi-Soviet Pact. Poland surrendered on September 28, remaining occupied until the end of the war.

The "Phoney War" followed, during which there were no major military operations in Western Europe. That ended on May 10, 1940, when Hitler's Wehrmacht (armed forces) launched invasions of Norway, Denmark, the Netherlands and Belgium, which were swiftly overrun. As the German Blitzkrieg (lightning war) swept through France, the British Expeditionary Force (BEF), along with French and Belgian troops, were forced to retreat to Dunkirk, where they were trapped on the beaches.

On May 25, the BEF's commander, Lord Gort, made the decision to evacuate. The shallow waters at Dunkirk prevented large ships from coming inshore, but in response to an Admiralty SOS, a fleet of 860 "small ships" came to the rescue, braving artillery and air attacks to ferry 338,000 Allied soldiers to safety. France surrendered on June 22. Although the consequence of military failure, the "Miracle of Dunkirk" greatly boosted British morale.

SIR WINSTON CHURCHILL
1874–1965; Prime Minister 1940–1945 and 1951–1955

Son of an aristocratic Tory politician and an American-born society beauty, Winston Churchill combined service in the army in India, Africa and on the Western Front with politics and journalism (as a war correspondent he escaped from a Boer prisoner-of-war camp). Originally a Conservative MP, he joined the Liberal Party in 1904, held several Cabinet posts, and pushed for major social reforms; as First Lord of the Admiralty he championed the disastrous Dardanelles campaign. Returning to the Tories in 1922, he was chancellor from 1924–1929, when the government fell. During ten years as a Conservative backbencher he became unpopular by opposing Indian self-government and supporting Edward VIII in the Abdication Crisis. He also warned of the Nazi threat, advocated rearmament and opposed Chamberlain's hesitant foreign policy.

Even his enemies acknowledged that Churchill would have to be brought into the government in the event of war. In 1939 he was reappointed First Lord of the Admiralty. Chamberlain's position became untenable after the Allied failure to protect Norway from German invasion (for which Churchill was partly responsible). With Germany advancing in Europe, Chamberlain's popularity plummeted and he resigned, to be replaced by Churchill on May 10, 1940, as Hitler's all-out war on the West began.

Forming a coalition government from all parties, Churchill proved a capable and inspirational wartime prime minister, and developed strong bonds with President Roosevelt and other foreign leaders. His defiance in defeat, coupled with his inspiring oratory and extraordinary energy, contributed significantly to the final Allied victory.

WAR IN THE AIR
August 13, 1940–May 8, 1944

Operation Sea Lion, Hitler's planned invasion of Britain, was to begin with the destruction of RAF Fighter Command. On August 13, 1940, Hermann Göring's Luftwaffe launched an all-out attack. The Battle of Britain had begun.

Fighting mainly over southern England, the RAF enjoyed tactical advantages in radar and with its superior fighter aircraft. Despite being heavily outnumbered, the pilots—many from occupied countries such as Poland—defended bravely, losing only 900 aircraft to the Luftwaffe's 1,700. Britain claimed victory on September 15. Two days later, Hitler postponed Sea Lion to concentrate on his secret plan to invade Russia.

Meanwhile, the Luftwaffe switched to attacking industrial production. The Blitz began on September 7, 1940, when 900 German aircraft bombed London's docks. Air raids came almost nightly until May 1941. Later, the Germans deployed guided missiles, although the Allies soon overran the launch sites.

Britain was prepared for the air raids with blackouts, people sleeping on Underground platforms and in shelters, and children evacuated from vulnerable cities. Despite widespread devastation, and the deaths of some 43,000 civilians, morale held.

It was not all one-sided: from 1942, RAF Bomber Command, led by Sir Arthur "Bomber" Harris, carried out a "saturation" night bombing campaign in Germany. After America entered the war, the USAF joined the campaign, flying precision attacks by day. By 1945, most German industrial centers had been destroyed or badly damaged, including the medieval city of Dresden, which was controversially devastated on February 13–15, killing 135,000 people.

WAR AT SEA
1940–1943

The "Battle of the Atlantic" lasted for most of the war, and was crucial for both sides. After the fall of France, Britain alone resisted the Nazis. The Atlantic Ocean was a lifeline, a route for American merchant ships bringing food, materials and military equipment to Britain. Unable to achieve air superiority, Hitler decided to attack Atlantic convoys so as to starve the British out, launching attacks in the summer of 1940 from newly gained territory in Norway and France. The First World War had proved submarines were effective, particularly for sabotaging supplies.

In early 1941, better convoy escorts and advances in radar reduced the damage done by submarines. The situation improved further when the Enigma codes were broken, allowing the British to discover U-boat positions. Although America was nominally neutral, it began to take an active part in defending the convoys, its navy allowed to sink U-boats on sight.

U-boat strength reached its peak in April 1942 when the Germans took advantage of American disorganization and new Enigma codes to wreak havoc. After major losses, the Allies prioritized anti-submarine defenses, and by May their air raids had destroyed many U-boats and their bases. Vice Admiral Dönitz ended the campaign in May 1943.

Thousands of Allied ships saw more than 100 convoy battles and 1,000 ship-to-ship fights in the vast Atlantic, and over 100,000 sailors were killed on both sides. Had the U-boats succeeded, Britain might well have been forced to surrender.

AMERICA ENTERS THE WAR
December 7, 1941

As Germany and Italy were fighting to occupy Europe and North Africa, and Japan was set to dominate China, the Far East and Australia, the United States remained neutral. Even though American interests were at stake, there was strong isolationist feeling among American voters and a series of neutrality laws restrained President Roosevelt from aggressive action.

However, Japan was uneasy about the American naval presence in the Pacific. Without warning, at dawn on December 7, 1941, two waves of Japanese carrier aircraft attacked the U.S. naval base at Pearl Harbor, Hawaii. Nine warships were sunk, twenty-one badly damaged, and almost 2,500 U.S. servicemen were killed.

Immediately Roosevelt went before Congress and requested a formal declaration of war against Japan. Three days later, Italy and Germany declared war on the United States. America was now fully involved in the war—a circumstance that was to ensure the eventual Allied victory.

Meanwhile, Britain was still heavily engaged in the Far East, despite being at full stretch fighting Hitler in Europe. In 1942, it suffered one of the most disastrous military campaigns in its history in the colony of Malaya (now part of Malaysia). British, Australian and Indian troops had been forced by the Japanese to retreat south down the Malayan peninsula to the "impregnable" island of Singapore. Fierce battles raged on land and in the air, but on February 15, 1942, Singapore was forced to surrender unconditionally. In the absence of an evacuation plan, about 80,000 Allied troops were stranded and made prisoners of war.

BLETCHLEY PARK AND ENIGMA
1939–1945

With the rise of radio communication, signals intelligence had become vital. During the Second World War, Germany relied mainly on a single code—Enigma.

Enigma was produced by cipher machines resembling typewriters. Messages were typed in and encoded by several notched rotors, which moved with each keystroke. This made conventional cryptology difficult, as the receiver had to know the daily changing settings.

In 1939, British Intelligence set up the top-secret project Ultra, with teams of cryptographers and mathematicians based at Bletchley Park. These included the mathematician Alan Turing, whose machines for calculating rotor settings were forerunners of the modern computer, and Polish refugees, whose prewar links to German engineering gave them understanding of the Enigma machine's workings.

The first code was broken in January 1940, but decryption remained difficult as ciphers changed. In early 1941 an Enigma machine, with books of rotor settings, was seized from a captured German trawler and taken for analysis by cryptographers, who realized that unarmed supply ships might all carry machines and books. The Navy focused its attacks and began to recover a steady stream of intelligence.

With the books, Bletchley Park could decrypt German messages fairly quickly, and Ultra provided the Allies with vital information about the German invasions of Greece and Russia (though Stalin refused to believe the latter), aiding Montgomery's North African campaign, including the victory at El Alamein in 1942. Ultra may have shortened the war by two years, but the secret was carefully guarded until the 1970s.

THE D-DAY LANDINGS AND VE DAY
June 6, 1944–May 8, 1945

By 1944, fighting had been concentrated on the Eastern Front for two years. A major European front was needed to reduce pressure on Russia (now an ally), so a plan was hatched for the Allies to invade the sheltered beaches of Normandy.

On June 6, Supreme Allied Commander Eisenhower caught the Germans off guard. At dawn, over 7,000 vessels, carrying 130,000 troops, departed for Normandy. The Germans' response was hindered by poor communications resulting from bombing and sabotage. Furthermore, they had been duped into expecting an invasion at Calais, and initially dismissed the Normandy landings as a diversion.

The 10,000 Allied casualties occurred mainly among U.S. troops at Omaha Beach, where amphibious tanks foundered. Evacuation was impossible, but naval support allowed the remaining troops to struggle heroically up the beach and overrun the defenses.

Hugely successful against the odds, D-day was the crucial beginning of European liberation. An Allied advance swept through Europe, retaking France and Belgium despite a setback at Arnhem, while another force invaded Italy. In the east, the Russians advanced through Poland. On April 30, 1945, Hitler killed himself in his bunker, two days after Mussolini's execution in Milan. On May 8, 1945, the Allies accepted Germany's unconditional surrender.

VE Day marked the end of war in Europe after five years, eight months and five days, to widespread jubilation. But austerity and rationing would persist for years, and there was a profound sadness at the events of the war. Tens of millions were dead, cities had been devastated, and the horrors of the Holocaust had been revealed.

VICTORY OVER JAPAN AND THE END OF THE SECOND WORLD WAR

August 15, 1945

War still raged in the east. The "forgotten" British 14th Army stationed in Burma was demoralized after crushing losses to the Japanese. However, the efforts of its commander, General Sir William Slim, in tackling the supply problems and training his troops in the art of jungle warfare paid off: By March 1945, Mandalay was recaptured and Rangoon fell to the Allied British and Indian forces in May. The Allies were ready to reverse their losses in Southeast Asia and were planning a massive invasion of Japan.

On August 6, however, news broke of a massive explosion over Hiroshima. An atomic bomb called "Little Boy" had been dropped on the instructions of President Truman, with a second bomb, "Fat Man," unleashed on Nagasaki three days later. Japan had rejected the terms of the Potsdam Declaration issued by Truman on July 26: "Surrender or suffer prompt and utter destruction." The effect of using nuclear weapons was unprecedented: In total, as many as 220,000 Japanese civilians died immediately, and countless others were to suffer from radiation illnesses. On August 10, the Soviet Union invaded Manchuria as part of its declaration of war on Japan, and on August 15, Japan was forced to surrender unconditionally, the last Axis enemy to do so. Emperor Hirohito (declaring to his shocked people that he was not, after all, a god) announced that the Japanese instrument of surrender had been signed on September 2, 1945 on board the battleship USS *Missouri*.

The Second World War was over.

THE FOUNDING OF THE UNITED NATIONS
1945

The founding mission of the United Nations was to maintain world peace and international dialogue in the light of the League of Nations' failure to avert the Second World War.

The name "United Nations" was first used by Churchill and Roosevelt to refer to the Allies, and first formally used in January 1942 in the Declaration by the United Nations. This was an agreement signed by an alliance of twenty-six governments that its members would unite in seeking peace deals with the Axis powers of Nazi Germany, Fascist Italy and Imperial Japan, rather than agreeing to separate peace deals.

After the experience of the Second World War, President Roosevelt decided America should lead the efforts of the United Nations for international peace and diplomacy. In consequence, the first United Nations Organization meeting took place in San Francisco on April 25, 1945, and fifty of the fifty-one member nations signed up to the United Nations' Charter at its headquarters in New York City on June 26, 1945 (Poland, which was not represented at the meeting, signed later). The first meeting of the General Assembly of the UN was held in the Methodist Central Hall, London, on January 10, 1946, attended by representatives of fifty-one nations. There are currently 192 member states.

FURTHER READING

A History of the English-Speaking Peoples by Sir Winston Churchill, Cassell, 4 volumes, 1956–1958

The Penguin Illustrated History of Britain and Ireland edited by Barry Cunliffe, Robert Bartlett, John Morrill, Asa Briggs and Joanna Bourke, Penguin, 2004

A History of Britain by Richard Dargie, Arcturus, 2007

A People's History of Britain by Rebecca Fraser, Pimlico, 2003

A Little History of the World by E.H. Gombrich, Yale University Press, 2005

The Oxford Illustrated History of Britain edited by Kenneth O. Morgan, Oxford University Press, 1984

INDEX

(page numbers in bold indicate main entries;
page numbers in *italic* indicate illustrations)